Outsmart Anxiety

A Self-Help Guide to Get Rid of Panic Attacks, Worry, and Fear

François J. Camus

© Copyright 2022 - All rights reserved.

The content contained within this book may not be reproduced, duplicated or transmitted without direct written permission from the author or the publisher.

Under no circumstances will any blame or legal responsibility be held against the publisher, or author, for any damages, reparation, or monetary loss due to the information contained within this book, either directly or indirectly.

Legal Notice:

This book is copyright protected. It is only for personal use. You cannot amend, distribute, sell, use, quote or paraphrase any part, or the content within this book, without the consent of the author or publisher.

Disclaimer Notice:

Please note the information contained within this document is for educational and entertainment purposes only. All effort has been executed to present accurate, up to date, reliable, complete information. No warranties of any kind are declared or implied. Readers acknowledge that the author is not engaged in the rendering of legal, financial, medical or professional advice. The content within this book has been derived from various sources. Please consult a licensed professional before attempting any techniques outlined in this book.

By reading this document, the reader agrees that under no circumstances is the author responsible for any losses, direct or indirect, that are incurred as a result of the use of the information contained within this document, including, but not limited to, errors, omissions, or inaccuracies.

Contents

Introduction 1
   A Gradual Decline in Wellness
   Finding Relief in Understanding Your Symptoms
   The Relevance of My Experience

1. Anxiety—Understanding What You Are Facing 9
   What Is Anxiety?
   How Common Is Anxiety?
   Anxiety Is Normal
   How Anxiety Affects Us
   Anxiety Can Become a Habit
   Anxiety Can Also Be an Addiction
   The Common Symptoms of Anxiety
   Anxiety Isn't All Bad
   The Benefits of Fear
   Takeaway

2. The Development of the Anxious Mind 29
   What Is the Anxious Mind?
   What Affects Your Mind?
   How Mindsets Are Formed

      Perceptions—Always a Concerning Matter
      Takeaway

3. How to Improve the Mind   45
      Exploring Happiness
      Seek Clarity to Change Your Self-Image
      Changing Your Mindset
      Understanding the Anxiety Cycle
      Old Habits Can Be Hard to Break
      Activities That Improve the Mind
      Takeaway

4. How to Improve Your Gut Health   63
      Microbiome
      Keeping the Gut Healthy Through Nutrition
      The Impact Your Eating Habits Have on Your Gut Health
      Exploring Gut Microbiota, the Intestinal Barrier, and the Immune System
      Various Popular Dietary Habits and Microbiota
      Foods That Are Harmful to the Gut Environment
      Food That Feeds the Soul—And the Gut
      Takeaway

5. Mind-Body Connection   81
      What Is the Mind-Body Connection?
      How Does the Mind-Body Connection Work?
      Exercise as an Aid to Alleviate Anxiety
      Yoga as an Aid to Alleviate Anxiety

Meditation as an Aid to Alleviate Anxiety
Takeaway

6. Forging New Habits   97
    Understanding Neuroplasticity
    Exploring How Habits Hardwire Your Brain
    What Is the Habit Loop?
    Pavlov's Dogs
    Changing Your Brain's Wiring Through Behavioral Changes
    Creating New Habit Loops in a Few Easy Steps
    Minimize Your Stress Levels
    Be More Mindful
    Take Small but Consistent Steps
    Boost Your Serotonin Levels
    Make Your Life a Priority You Think About
    Celebrate More Often
    Take Stock of Your Crowd
    Takeaway

7. Professional Solutions and Limits   113
    Exploring Psychotherapy
    Cognitive Behavioral Therapy
    Exposure Therapy
    Medication
    Other Medication
    The Limits of Medical Treatment Options
    Addressing Anxiety Symptoms

Takeaway

8. Support Network — 129
   How to Find a Support Group
   Benefits of a Support Network
   Exploring the Structure of a Support Group
   You Should Support Yourself Too
   When Should You Build Your Support Network?
   How to Strengthen Your Support Network
   Takeaway

9. Coping Techniques — 137
   Using Breathing
   Combining Breathing and Smiling
   Use Your Senses to Calm Yourself Down
   Using Mindfulness
   Get to Know Your Anger
   Indulge in Fun
   Turn Off Your Mind
   Consistently Bring Back Your Wandering Mind
   Stop Worrying Indefinitely
   Address the Causes of Your Anxiety
   Affirmations
   Using Diversions
   Diversion Techniques Defined
   The Five Best Diversion Techniques
   Takeaway

10. Conclusion — 152

A Free eBook to Our Readers

Discover the proven techniques that have a direct impact on your body and mind, and **bring your relaxation to the next level.**

gift.mindoutsmarter.com

Introduction

Last year, the total number of people diagnosed with anxiety disorder globally came to a staggering 284 million (Dattani et al., 2021). Over half of this group are women, though anxiety doesn't give preference to any age group. It may be more predominant in those aged 30–45, but it is also prevalent in children as young as 3 (Centers for Disease Control and Prevention [CDC], n.d.).

Still, many more than what these numbers reflect are suffering in silence. They haven't been able to connect the dots to realize that the symptoms they experience are all linked to increased anxiety levels. As a result, the many techniques and coping mechanisms available to bring the relief they so desperately desire are still unknown to them. Are you maybe one of these unrecorded cases?

A Gradual Decline in Wellness

It can be hard to exactly pinpoint what you feel. There are specific symptoms like a racing pulse, dizziness, excessive sweating, feeling disconnected from your body, nausea, and vomiting, to name some symptoms. But how do you put in words the feelings it leaves with you at that moment… and long afterward?

It may feel so unexpected when it all comes crashing in. Nonetheless, it also wasn't out of the blue at all. If you are honest, you've been aware of the emotional buildup over the past couple of months, the endless worrying that just won't stop. You've felt like an elastic being pulled and pulled daily, and you've wondered how much further you could go. Yet, you dare not show weakness as you've been waiting for this moment for your entire career. Now is your time to shine in your professional and personal life.

Furthermore, you have also battled with the painful reality of knowing that something will give in. The entire time, though, you thought the immense stress you are lately dealing with would subside. Not once did you think it would be your system that came crashing down so abruptly. You didn't even realize what it was when it happened, nor can you identify the final trigger that sent you over the edge.

Where were you when it first hit you where it hurts? Sitting behind your desk at work? Cooking for your family in the kitchen? Perhaps while presenting your proposal to a major client? Initially, you were not sure what was happening. Your heart was pumping rapidly, and then you thought you were having a heart attack. Your mouth was so dry, and you wanted to get some water, but as you got up, dizziness hit you quickly, turning into nausea.

After throwing up, you felt a little better. Leaning back against the bathroom wall, you realize you are dripping with sweat. You felt tired and drained, but above all, it was the feeling of being scared that got your attention. Did you just almost die?

Finding Relief in Understanding Your Symptoms

It doesn't matter how your journey with anxiety started. How or when it turned into something you could no longer suppress to deal with later is unique to all. What is essential, though, is not to allow this to threaten your overall health and wellness any longer than necessary, so that you don't postpone taking action anymore. You must step up and take back control over your life as what you've just experienced was anxiety steering your destiny, and that is not a pleasant way to live.

The first thing you need to know about anxiety is that even if you feel incredibly isolated, you are not alone. Many others are facing the same challenges as you, and there are many places and people keen to assist you on your healing journey.

Then, you must shift your focus and realize that this is not the end of your journey; rather, you've reached a crossroads in your life. What has happened to you may happen again and again until you decide to address the matter. What happened was that your body refused to be ignored any longer. It stated that it had enough, signaling your need to step up and make your health and wellness a priority in your life.

The good news is that you can turn the entire situation around. You can become well and confident again, as well as lead a brilliant and relaxed life, after overcoming anxiety. I've witnessed many people plummeting to the ground, like you did, throughout my career. I've seen the agony they put themselves and their loved ones through; and, I've also seen how many of them have turned their lives around.

Anxiety is a growing global concern. The human body is designed to function optimally in highly stressful circumstances, but it is not intended to remain under immense stress for extended periods. Initially, it will cry out for help, but if ignored, the mind and body simply crash and burn. However, we are resilient, and we survive.

In this book, I am sharing all the information I've gathered through years of research and close observation, guiding you to live the life you've dreamed about. First, we place anxiety under the microscope to explore it in its most delicate details and to truly grasp an understanding of what we are up against. Then, we'll become familiar with the mind and how it works to ensure that we effectively employ this part of our being.

Throughout the rest of the book, our focus will also be on how the mind and body are complexly intertwined and how you can't heal one without addressing the needs of the other. As a result of this intricate bond between mind and body, anxiety affects several areas of your existence. By knowing and understanding the more significant complexities of our being, we can dig deeper into our identity, perceptions, and beliefs. This in-depth search allows us to witness a range of solutions and opportunities unfold to counter and alleviate the impact of anxiety.

You can also create significant changes in your life by making minor changes to your habits. You'll learn how to master this technique and build a structure in your personal and professional life that can support your new approach to health and well-being. I will share vital information on relieving the symptoms you are experiencing through changing your diet and making gut health a priority with the valuable aid of nutrition.

Are you curious to learn what options are available when you want to call on professional expertise for assistance? We'll also go into great depth into these possibilities and familiarize ourselves with the limitations in this regard. Often, long after leaving your professional expert's practice, your support network and coping techniques make life more bearable, enjoyable, and fun. So, we'll explore how you can make the most of these opportunities.

You may be in a dark state now, feeling lost, confused, and, above all, mentally and emotionally tired and overwhelmed. Yet, I want you to remain aware that there is always hope as we proceed. Always maintain your focus on the fact that you are getting better. While you may be moving in tiny increments, progress is better than perfection as long as you are moving forward.

The Relevance of My Experience

For years, I've been withnessing the impact of anxiety on people, their relationships, careers, and every other aspect of their lives, robbing them of a sense of joy and fulfillment. But, my research also covered healing and how the many techniques available for overcoming these challenges. I've witnessed how people regained control over their lives, restored family bonds, and how careers flourished again. This triggered a passion, a passion driven by knowing that while the tunnel may feel long and dark, there is light shining brighter than ever before once you've found your way to the other side. The recovery and healing I saw so often inspired me and motivated me to share the light side of anxiety with you.

Are you ready to explore new solutions to this ancient concern? Do you want to follow my guidance as I share previously unexplored techniques, coping mechanisms, habits, and dietary adjustments toward the end of the darkness? Do you feel it is time to cut ties from living this way?

Let's take that first step on your journey towards the other side so you can walk away as the victor over anxiety.

Chapter One

Anxiety—Understanding What You Are Facing

Knowing others is intelligence; knowing yourself is true wisdom. Mastering others is strength; mastering yourself is true power. –Lao Tzu

Sometimes, it happens that a word turns into a buzzword, while a large part of users don't have an accurate understanding of what the word means. Anxiety is an excellent example of such a word. Thus, before we further explore the many ways you can approach anxiety and regain control over your life, we need to make a pit stop first—we need to delve deeper into the meaning of anxiety, and how it impacts your life and the lives of your loved ones.

What Is Anxiety?

According to the American Psychological Association, "anxiety is an emotion characterized by feelings of tension, worried thoughts, and physical changes like increased blood pressure" (APA, n.d. para 1).

Some would refer to anxiety as a normal, essential emotion. When we experience anxiety, our brains alert us and prepare us physically to defend ourselves from any potential danger. Your heart starts to beat faster, ensuring enough oxygen gets to your muscles so that you can fight off a threat or run fast enough to escape with your life.

During ancient times before civilization, anxiety might have been the body's response that kept your ancestors alive. Thanks to anxiety, humankind managed to survive and evolve, and it kept us from becoming extinct. Imagine a time when people had to hunt for their food—they had to leave the safety of their caves and venture into the jungle. Every time they went out into the jungle, they would be the hunter or the hunted. If they wanted to return safely, they would have to be on high alert the entire time, ready to fend off any predator jumping from its concealed hiding spot in the jungle. The world that was their home had many predators to face, and if you were not careful and alert to your environment the entire time, you might just not make it home.

Under these circumstances, anxiety is good; it is a defense mechanism that helps you to survive. While the body is excellently adjusted to deal with high anxiety levels during these intervals, it is not designed to be exposed to anxiety over long periods. Anxiety becomes a significant concern when we experience all these physical reactions triggered by our mental state while not being exposed to any actual danger. Then, we are no longer only talking about anxiety but are referring to generalized anxiety disorder (GAD).

How Common Is Anxiety?

Throughout the book, I need you to remember that you are not alone. When your anxiety levels become unbearable, it can be easy to feel isolated. There are millions of people across the globe going through the same challenges as you are. Exposure to lasting stress and anxiety is a significant concern affecting 1 out of 14 people on earth (Remes, 2017). Statistics from the National Alliance on Mental Illness (NAMI, 2017) indicate that in the United States alone, 40 million people suffer from an anxiety disorder—this makes up 19.1% of the population. We also learn that it is not only an adult concern, as 7% of children between the ages of 3–17 also suffer from anxiety symptoms.

Anxiety Is Normal

Anxiety is a perfectly normal experience that everyone has at some stage in their lives. Imagine waking up in the middle of the night to a strange noise, and you don't know what it is. Maybe it is an intruder in your house, or perhaps the neighbor's cat is again visiting the garbage bins in your yard. For a few seconds, you can even hear your racing heart beating in your ears. Your mouth is dry, and you are almost too scared to breathe. Then, you slowly get up, careful not to make a sound. Before you go downstairs to confront whoever is in your home, you peek through the window; you see him—the cat you dread. This time, you feel a sense of relief to see him, though. His presence confirms that there is indeed nothing to fear. Your heart stops racing and returns to its normal pace. You are much more relaxed now, but now that you are awake, you figure you might as well go downstairs and make yourself a nice cup of tea before returning to bed. You walk downstairs relaxed as your body returns to its normal state.

What you've experienced just now was anxiety. We feel anxiety when we are scared, threatened, or when we get frightened. Essentially anxiety is nothing but a physical reaction to a stimulus that starts in the brain. The purpose of the trigger is to protect you from perceived danger. As a result, you'll be able to overcome the challenge you face more effectively. So, anxiety protects us from possible danger.

How Anxiety Affects Us

Being anxious affects our thoughts, body, and behaviors. This attribute of anxiety is how it keeps us alive. Let's revisit our ancestors' hunting in the jungle and explore the setting closely. When the hunters left their caves to find food, they constantly thought about all the dangers surrounding them. Many of these dangers were so well camouflaged that you'd never see them until they had jumped right on you. Remember that these hunters were as much facing the possibility of being the prey to a roaming predator as they were hunters themselves. Thinking about all the dangers they were facing kept them in a state of anxiety.

The state of anxiety left them with dilated pupils that enabled them to see with greater clarity. Their muscles were tense, so they could react to any danger much faster and stronger than expected. Their elevated heart rate pushed more oxygen to their muscles, allowing them to fight to the end. The presence of anxiety triggers the secretion of adrenaline, allowing us to run faster, jump higher, and continue for longer than we ever can without it.

Anxiety can also be very bad for us. The problem we face in the modern world we live in is that we experience the same levels of anxiety as our ancestors, but ours is different—it doesn't end. Their adrenaline levels dropped to normal again once the anxiety-provoking situation had passed. Our levels remain high, as what causes us to experience anxiety is not a threat that is merely there for a moment and then gone.

We enter the public sphere and are anxious that something may happen to us. Our newspapers are filled with stories about increased crime rates, murders, and violence in our streets. So, you may walk in the street and be constantly aware of the dangers lurking around you. Once you enter your home, your anxiety levels should drop to normal again, like the ancient hunters did when they returned to their caves, but it doesn't. Once home, other things are contributing to your anxiety. Now, your mind is consumed with retrenchments at work, pressing deadlines, a challenging economic climate, and fear that you may lose your house. As none of these causes of your anxiety blows over, it keeps you in a constant state of elevated anxiety levels. Your anxiety is now a matter of concern.

The following conditions indicate that your anxiety has turned into a problem:

- When innocent events happen, like a vehicle breaking rapidly outside your window, it increases your anxiety.

- When the above type of situation occurs often.

- When you find that the level of anxiety you experience becomes more intense.

- When anxiety keeps you from doing the things you enjoy in life and what is important to you.

Anxiety Can Become a Habit

Habits are seemingly insignificant actions that we keep busy with and hardly ever notice that we are doing it. Some habits are good and can benefit your life in many ways; examples of such habits would be brushing your teeth after eating, drinking plenty of water, or ensuring that you get enough hours of sleep every night. We also have habits that are very bad for us: biting our nails; snacking late at night and then going to sleep on a full stomach; or indulging anxiety as part of our lives.

When anxiety has become a habit in your life, you find yourself in a sticky situation. This is mainly the case because habits can be hard to shed. We are so used to turning to our habits that we don't realize that it is an automated response. You can calm yourself down during an offset of anxiety by deep breathing while getting through the moment; yet, we can't shed habits in this manner.

When we want to learn more about how anxiety turns into a habit, we need to turn our attention to the research and findings of Dr. John Brewer. He explains that habits are formed in three steps (2021): First, there is a trigger or cue. Second, there is an action or behavior. And third, from a brain perspective, there is a reward. For example, anxiety is unpleasant. That could be the cue. The behavior related to the cue could be physical, like eating, or mental, like worrying. The truth is, worrying has become a huge habit for those with anxiety because it gives a false sense of control. Even if somebody can't change a situation, at least they feel like they're doing something constructive by remaining active instead of inactive. Whether it is physical or mental, that behavior gives them a sense of accomplishment that becomes a reward for the brain.

As we can now see how habits and anxiety are linked, we'll explore how you can change your habits to overcome anxiety in a later chapter.

Anxiety Can Also Be an Addiction

As experiencing anxiety can be such an unpleasant experience, it can be hard to fathom how anyone would be addicted to it. However, we can say the same about climbing skyscrapers just for fun or jumping off a cliff to enjoy the rush of adrenaline through your veins. Dr. Judith Orloff (2011) explains that just as people are addicted to the thrill of adrenaline they get when they take part in extreme sports, some also are addicted to the rush they get when they experience an anxiety attack.

She shares the following questions to help determine if you are addicted to anxiety:

1. Do you worry about things daily?

2. Do you struggle to switch the channel and watch something other than the anxiety-provoking news on TV?

3. Do you feel anxious when you aren't near your phone or computer?

4. Do you often exaggerate problems rather than play them down?

5. Do you find yourself stressing over things nobody else

ever worries about?

6. Do you find that once one concern is resolved, you simply jump to the next point to worry over?

Affirmative answers to all six of these questions would clearly indicate that you are addicted to the role that anxiety plays in your life.

Here, too, it would be much harder to simply free yourself from anxiety as you are no longer merely dealing with the emotions and the physical response of anxiety, but you also have to approach the matter similarly to any other approach to addiction recovery.

The Common Symptoms of Anxiety

While several anxiety symptoms are present across all types of anxiety disorders, the symptoms mostly vary according to the type of disorder.

Generalized Anxiety Disorder

Those suffering from generalized anxiety disorder usually experience a persistent state of anxiety or constant dread that something terrible will happen. This state can become so severe that it will interrupt their daily living. Do not confuse this state with the regular bouts of worry everyone experiences; the level of anxiety of those who suffer from GAD is constant and severe, and it continues for months. In some cases, the state can last for years.

The symptoms commonly associated with GAD are

- restlessness, being on edge or feeling agitated.
- you may struggle to concentrate.
- a heightened sense of irritability.
- you may feel tired quickly.
- your worrying is out of control.
- you may suffer from headaches, muscle pain, and even an upset stomach.
- you have a hard time falling asleep, or you will wake up often during the night.

Panic Disorder

Panic attacks can be scary, and the worst is that you never know when they will happen. The uncertainty about when you will be triggered again is one of the most concerning aspects to many who have panic disorder. It is why many would try to avoid certain places which they feel may cause them to get a panic attack. This can be very limiting to your life. However, even by avoiding certain places, you have no certainty that you won't get triggered and experience a panic attack in places you deem safe. It can also be challenging to identify the triggers that put you into this state of panic.

It is important that I emphasize that you don't necessarily have panic disorder if you've experienced one or two panic attacks. A diagnosis of panic disorder requires regular and severe panic attacks over an extended period. Some people diagnosed with panic disorder may only experience panic attacks a couple of times a year; for others, it can become so severe that they have several panic attacks daily.

The most common symptoms people experience when they have a panic attack are

- an elevated heart rate.
- excessive sweating.
- chest pain.
- difficulty breathing.
- trembling, dizziness, and tingling all over their bodies.
- feeling a sense of being entirely out of control.
- feeling disconnected from themselves.
- being plagued by fears of impending doom that they can't prevent.

Phobia-Related Disorders

There are more than 400 recognized phobias worldwide ("Surprising Facts About Phobias," n.d.). Phobias refer to an extreme fear of a specific situation or object; examples of phobias are

- acrophobia—fear of heights.
- aviophobia—fear of flying.
- agoraphobia—a fear of crowded public places.
- claustrophobia—a fear of enclosed rooms.

Phobias are related to intense but ungrounded fear. The situation or object linked to the phobia doesn't pose any risk to the person who has the phobia.

Those who suffer from a specific phobia experience the following symptoms:

- They have an irrational and ungrounded fear of coming across the object or situation.
- They often go to severe lengths to avoid the situation.
- They experience extreme anxiety when they encounter the thing or situation they fear.

We can also divide phobias into different categories. The most common type of phobias is specific phobias, also known as simple phobias. Simple phobias refer to a fear linked to a particular object or situation; they include the fear of flying, heights, spiders, injections, and even the fear of blood.

A more complex type of phobia is agoraphobia. The condition refers to a state where people would fear two or more different types of objects or situations from the following:

- fearing to use public transport.
- fear of being in open spaces—or being in enclosed spaces.
- fear of standing in lines.
- avoiding being in crowds.
- the fear of being alone outside of their homes.

Those with agoraphobia would do anything to avoid finding themselves in a situation where they have to face their fears. What makes these fears even worse is the fear that they will embarrass themselves if they had a panic attack in a crowd. The fear of humiliation caused by a panic attack triggered by these conditions worsens this phobia. Therefore, it is common for those with agoraphobia to remain housebound for most of their lives.

Social Anxiety Disorder

Social anxiety disorder is linked to anxiety people may experience in social situations. These people are often plagued by the idea that someone is constantly watching and judging them. As a result, they will obsess over many things they fear they may do in a social situation that may cause them severe humiliation, instilling an intense fear that just doesn't pass. They may have no control over their behavior in social settings, so these moments invest immense fear in them. Therefore, they avoid situations where many might gather and where they may have to interact with other people. It may sound simple enough to avoid social gatherings, but many other situations are sources for this fear too. Those suffering from a social anxiety disorder struggle attending school and going to shops—even a busy day on the beach can be too much for them.

The most common symptoms people experience when they have social anxiety disorder are

- a racing heartbeat.

- excessive sweating, trembling and blushing.

- a rigid body posture, almost coming across as being

stiff.

- speaking overly softly.

- stomach pain and an upset stomach.

- struggling to make eye contact.

- being very self-conscious.

- constantly fearing the judgment and criticism of others

Separation Anxiety Disorder

This condition is mainly linked to toddlers going through a stage where they can't be separated from their parents. When these children don't see their parents, they react with emotional and uncontrollable outbursts. While it is pretty common for toddlers to experience this fear, they mostly grow out of it. However, separation anxiety disorder is also a concern for many adults. Adults suffering from separation anxiety disorder have an intense fear of being separated from someone they are attached to. They will do anything not to be alone and to stay close to this person. This fear is so overwhelming that even when they sleep, they may have nightmares of being separated from this person.

Understandably, this fear creates a very challenging situation for the person with the phobia and the one they are attached to. It generates the same physical symptoms as most other anxiety disorders, which usually surface as soon as the person suffering from this disorder becomes aware of the fact that they will be separated from the person they are attached to. Because of this dynamic, separation anxiety disorder impacts not only the person it plagues, but it also impacts those close to them.

Anxiety Isn't All Bad

Now that we've covered a broad overview of anxiety and what it entails, I want to highlight the idea that experiencing fear is not always bad. It would be wrong to constantly perceive fear in a negative light. Like with most other things in life, fear or anxiety also have a place and a purpose in the world.

Before we explore the beneficial roles that fear and anxiety have to play, I want to expand a little bit more on eustress. Researchers refer to eustress as positive stress (Scott, 2022). It is the kind of stress we experience that delivers a positive response. Eustress only presents itself for short periods; examples of this stress include starting a new job, going on a roller coaster ride, or traveling to a foreign country. Like the usual stress we know, it can bring about an increased heart rate as well as other symptoms commonly linked to being in distress. However, when people experience eustress, they feel it is manageable; feeling good, even excited, is expected once the fear has passed. Eustress is a version of fear that passes quickly, is manageable, and leaves us feeling great.

The Benefits of Fear

Let's explore what benefits you can enjoy from fear and anxiety.

Anxiety Warns Us of Danger

Just like anxiety helped our ancestors to survive the threats they were exposed to in the jungle and to keep humankind from extinction, fear can also be safe from trauma, injury, or any other form of distress. When you become aware of either fear or anxiety in your life, it is best not to ignore it but rather to determine what it is trying to warn you against. Maybe you find yourself in the company of someone you shouldn't trust, or you are in a career that is so draining that, if you don't get out soon, you may collapse under the stress it puts on you. When walking to your car in a deserted parking lot, anxiety puts you on high alert to ensure you get to your vehicle safely. Fear and anxiety can save your life. Don't ignore it when it presents itself.

Fear and Anxiety Motivates Us to Create Change

Change is very hard to establish in our lives. We often underestimate how difficult change can be. As change demands that we step outside of our comfort zones, we hardly find enough motivation to do so unless our situation becomes so unbearable that we have no other choice. In these cases, it is fear and anxiety that drives change.

For example, let's say you need to lose a lot of weight, but you just simply can't get yourself to make the changes you need to improve your health. Then one day, your doctor tells you that if you don't lose a certain amount of weight soon, you will most likely not survive to see your children grow up. Now, you are faced with the fear of dying and leaving your children to be orphans. This fear motivates you to make the changes you need to make, drop that extra weight, and survive.

It Is Our Built-In Alarm System Keeping Us From Danger

Fear is the trigger behind the fight-or-flight response. Several years ago, the local paper featured an article about a near abduction of a local teenager walking home after dark. The girl stated that she felt like someone was watching her the entire time and felt anxious to get home. Suddenly, a car pulled up next to her and tried to kidnap her. In the car were three guys—one grabbed her arm, and, in a brave response, she managed to kick the guy in the face and pull herself loose from his grip. As her body was pumping with adrenaline, she managed to run away so fast that she escaped. A few weeks later, another girl was grabbed, but she was less fortunate. Fortunately, the criminals were caught shortly after. Everyone was talking about the bravery of the girl who managed to escape. However, if it wasn't for the fact that fear had already made her alert, she may not have been able to be so successful in her fight-or-flight response to the attack.

Fear Inspires Greater Empathy

Being familiar with the impact of fear and how it can affect your life tends to make people far more empathetic in their personal relationships. It is common for these people to better understand the challenges that others experience, and they provide adequate emotional support to those in need.

It Makes Stronger Leaders

We all need to make choices from time to time in our lives that can have an immense impact on our future. Leaders have to make these choices almost daily, though the effect of their choices doesn't only affect their lives but also the lives of many others. Thus, when you are a leader, you always need to be more alert to the potential impact of your decisions. This awareness, driven by anxiety and fear of making the wrong choices, helps leaders to be better at what they do. It inspires them to consider far more factors before making their final decision.

Now, we have explored anxiety and fear from every possible angle. It is time to see how we can cure the anxious mind and manage fear and anxiety so that it can benefit you.

Takeaway

Anxiety is a normal feeling that we all experience at some time in our lives. It is beneficial to help us survive and was a great asset for our ancestors to prevent them from becoming extinct. However, the modern society we live in has many triggers that cause us to feel the same levels of anxiety as our ancestors did. The concern is that the threats causing our bodies to enter a fight-or-flight mode aren't life-threatening and are not temporary. When the human body is exposed to high levels of stress for extended times, many things start to go wrong—anxiety and depression are merely two of such outcomes. As we become more familiar with anxiety and its origins, causes, contributing factors, and cycle, we can employ many solutions to address the concern effectively. It is how you can reclaim your life and live the life you dream about.

Chapter Two

The Development of the Anxious Mind

> If you change the way you look at things, the things you look at change. –*Wayne W. Dyer*

It's no secret that anxiety can be a crippling force in someone's life. What is less commonly known, however, is the way anxiety affects the mind and how it can lead to negative perceptions. In this chapter, we will explore the anxious mind in detail and how it can impede creativity and productivity.

Before exploring the contributing factors to the anxious mind and how it all happens, we first need to determine what the anxious mind is.

What Is the Anxious Mind?

The anxious mind is the mind constantly reminding you that you need to be concerned and alert, and that you are in the presence of imminent danger. It could save your life if you were facing actual life-threatening danger, but you're not—you are perfectly fine in the present moment. Yes, you have to pay bills at the end of the month, and you have no idea how your child will pass this academic year, but these concerns are locked in the future. You do regret buying that expensive pair of boots which is extremely uncomfortable, and now you will most likely be short on your rent, but that is in the past. In the present moment—reading, standing, cooking for your family, or working on a deadline due tomorrow—nothing is threatening your life. You are in no danger at all. Even so, your anxious mind won't let go and will keep you on high alert. Every muscle in your body is strung tight… and it is all based on a convincing lie. That lie tells you that you must protect yourself and remain in fight-or-flight mode the entire time.

What Affects Your Mind?

Our entire life is shaped by a collection of experiences from the moment we are born. These experiences are sometimes good, and other times they may be bad. Each of these experiences helps to shape our minds. The influence they have is determined by the severity of the impact they have on our consciousness.

Self-Image

Self-image refers to your mental picture of yourself when you think about who you are. It can be positive, negative, or balanced. It will include what you think about your physical appearance, talents, skills, level of intelligence, and popularity, to name only some of the pieces that construct your self-image. In a way, it is how you judge your capabilities in every possible aspect of existence, deeming yourself as excellent, average, or terrible, and every other point on the ratio in between.

It is a primary building block in human personality and behavior; if you change this image of yourself, you change your entire nature and usual behavior. By changing this part of your being, you can change who you are regardless of how old you are. In my experience, it is never too early or too late to change. You always have the freedom to make different choices that better suit the life you desire. This is my first observation regarding self-image.

Another notable point is that everything you do—your behavior, ideas, beliefs, words, actions, and abilities—always aligns with your image of yourself. This reaffirms the concept that you hold the power when defining who you are or want to be. Consequently, our self-image lies within our hands.

So, if you have an anxious mind, it, too, will be aligned with the image you have of who you are, as your self-image impacts your mindset.

Mindset

It is not the only way your mindset is formed, though. No, several factors impact how your mindset is formed over time. Your mindset is a list of benchmarks, definitions, or explanations that you use to make sense of the world surrounding you. Your mindset is your reference point in the world that can sometimes be overwhelming and confusing. As mindset plays such a vital role, we need to determine how the mindset forms, evolves and expands. It is how we can change our mindsets to perceive the world differently.

How Mindsets Are Formed

We can distinguish between two types of mindsets: a fixed mindset and a growth mindset. The predominant feature of a fixed mindset that positions it apart from a growth mindset is that whatever one states is set in stone and can never be changed. In contrast, a growth mindset considers every challenge an opportunity to grow and better yourself. It believes that we can constantly develop our intelligence and abilities.

The Impact of the Environment

The environment you find yourself in contributes largely to the type of mindset you host. When referring to the environment, it is crucial to know that it is an umbrella term for various factors: news, past outcomes, education, religion, culture, socioeconomic circumstances, and more. It can also refer to the type of feedback you get from others.

An example of a fixed mindset is when you hear your mother-in-law telling her friends that you are a terrible cook. She is an excellent chef, and you believe what she is saying because of the expertise to her name. Initially, her comments hurt you, but as time passes, you also start to think you are a terrible cook. Worse, you believe this will never change and that you'll always fail in the kitchen. As this is your mindset, you adjust your actions to align with your beliefs. Eventually, you become a terrible cook who would rather not set foot in a kitchen.

A growth mindset allows for perceptions to change over time. We can use the same example of your mother-in-law's comments—now, you don't take her word for the truth, as you can remember that you've received plenty of comments about your cooking in the past. However, given she has all these years of experience, you still want to change her perception of your cooking skills. You see her comments as an opportunity to improve your skills. Therefore, you take cooking classes, spend hours in the kitchen honing your skills, and change how she perceives your cooking ability. Those with a growth mindset believe that potential is unpredictable. You can look at life by seeing the glass as half empty or half full—the choice is always yours. This is not how those with a fixed mindset perceive themselves, though.

The Impact of Your Lifestyle

As body, mind, and soul are so connected, it is understandable that lifestyle choices greatly influence your mindset and impact your lifestyle. An unhealthy lifestyle is bound to lead to some serious mindset concerns. It robs you of enjoying a whole and happy life. You will likely struggle to identify what your strengths and weaknesses are and have limited resilience, if any. These are only some of the ways how your mindset impacts your lifestyle. On the other hand, if you sustain a healthy lifestyle, you can enjoy several mindset benefits. You focus better and for longer; improve the symptoms of anxiety and depression; have higher self-worth; and are in charge of your day as you're better equipped to structure your day effectively.

The Impact of Social Media

For years, researchers have been exploring the impact that social media has on our mindset. It is widely understood that spending a lot of time on social media platforms can lead to increased anxiety, feelings of isolation, depression, and even thoughts of self-harm. These platforms are designed to create a sense of inadequacy in our lives. The trap people step into is that they compare their lives with the lives of others present on these platforms. It creates an unfair playground as what gets shared on social media is not real. Nobody shares their mistakes, bad hair days, or days they feel down; instead, they share mostly "red carpet" moments to which you compare your ordinary days with. When you do, you are bound to fall short, leaving you with a negative mindset about your life.

The Impact of Sedentary Activities

The time when most careers entailed spending hours on your feet and walking a lot has passed. Today, technology demands that most of the workforce spend hours behind a computer screen. Recent research indicates that when people spend more than eight hours sitting behind a computer, it can impact their mental health severely. This is the case even when they are active for more than 150 minutes per week, doing moderate to vigorous exercise. While most of us can't just get up from our computers and spend time on our feet as we would like, it is essential to consider the impact of this kind of lifestyle when it comes to the state of our mindset.

The Impact of TV on Your Mindset

Television has always been an aid to help us relax and as a means to escape our troubles, even if it is only for a short while. Still, researchers struggled to determine the long-term impact of spending a lot of time in front of the TV. Over recent years, the number of hours of offline watching remained stable, but online watching has increased immensely, mainly a result of more young viewers spending endless hours online.

More recent studies now reveal that this behavior leads to higher rates of depression and feeling lonely or isolated. This isolation is prevalent regardless of the common belief that being online leaves users feeling connected. Constant exposure to the influx of information also negatively impacts neuron development in young children's brains. These children generally score lower on language tests and show slower thinking. While we all can become addicted to binge-watching on our smart devices, this remains a significant concern for younger users who are not yet able to distinguish when to draw the line and disconnect.

What you are watching will also, to a great extent, determine how watching TV impacts your mindset. Watching a comedy or losing yourself in a romantic display is one thing. In contrast, if it is the stressful doom and gloom of the news that is your constant feed, you are bound to experience an increase in anxiety, stress, and depression. Merely watching the news can cause you to feel similar emotions as the victims in the stories you observe. Naturally, your stress hormones will spike, feeding the anxious mind.

The Impact of Social Activities

Social activities and the level to which people are involved in their community and have access to support systems are widely considered beneficial to their mindset. Those who are often involved in social activities are less likely to feel isolated. When they do, it is easier to combat their sense of loneliness.

Being social improves your mood and leaves you feeling relaxed, inspired, positive, and motivated. The range of social activities you can get involved in to access these benefits is also rather vast. It offers enough choices to accommodate the needs of most.

The Impact of Romantic Relationships

Being in a healthy, happy, and loving romantic relationship can immensely benefit your mindset. The caring support and excitement of being in a romantic relationship often relieves symptoms of depression and anxiety and is a trusted way to overcome feelings of isolation (Adam, 2021). It provides a safe space to share your emotions, be vulnerable and feel valued and appreciated for who you are.

A healthy sex life is an added benefit to any relationship, as this, too, improves your mindset. But, note that the opposite is also the case, and mental concerns can adversely impact your sex life.

The Impact of Physical Touch

Humans are social beings, and we need physical touch to be happy and healthy. The lack of physical contact leads to a state called touch starvation. It occurs when there is a lack of any physical touch for an extended period. Touch starvation leads to increased levels of anxiety, depression, and stress. This is all caused by increased levels of cortisol. Cortisol, or the stress hormone, also causes an increased heart rate and blood pressure, muscle tension, and higher levels of inflammation. The science behind the phenomenon teaches us that the body releases oxytocin—known as the "love" hormone—when we are exposed to soft and soothing strokes on our skin's surface, reducing stress and improving our overall well-being.

The Impact of Work Satisfaction

We may try to keep our professional and personal lives separate. Still, we are human and spend a lot of time in the work environment, so what happens at this time is bound to affect our mindset. Here, too, you will find a strong correlation between the level of satisfaction you enjoy at the office and your mindset. Low levels of work satisfaction can lead to feeling burned out. It lowers your self-esteem and lessens the things you think you are capable of achieving. The opposite is also true: The more satisfaction you have in your work, the more your self-worth increases, empowering you to be happy and confident and to enjoy an overall sense of wellness.

The Impact of Proximity Effect

Jim Rohn first taught us that we become the average of the five people we spend most of our time with (Plano, n.d.). In this one statement, he summarized the entire proximity effect. The effect explains how we become more like the people we share our company with. If you are mostly surrounded by people with a general negative outlook on life, your perspective will also turn negative. But, if you spend your time with primarily positive people, showcasing a growth mindset, that is the direction you'll lean more toward instead. It is why it is essential to pick the company you keep discerningly.

The Impact of Addiction to Drugs or Alcohol

Regardless of what substance you are addicted to, it will harm your overall well-being. Those suffering from some kind of addiction often are far more stressed, have lower self-esteem, feel isolated, and are depressed. Addiction can also cause paranoia and is extremely disempowering. In some cases, substances can cause an increased sense of euphoria. Still, once this comes crashing down, it can lead to feeling anxious and stressed out.

The Impact of Direct Sunlight

Several hormones are closely linked to light and darkness. When exposed to high light conditions, your brain releases hormones that support your mindset to be more positive and relaxed. Low-light conditions have the opposite effect. This effect is typically visible on a much larger scale in countries that have fewer sunny days than others. When your retinas are exposed to sunlight, it serves as a trigger to release higher levels of serotonin, leaving you feeling happy and cheerful. When these serotonin levels drop, you are more likely to feel depressed and anxious. The role of sunlight in sustaining overall mental wellness is so influential that sunlight is even used as a form of therapy. Light boxes are utilized in countries with less sunlight to bring relief to those suffering from depression and anxiety.

The Impact of Sleep Routines

Sleep and anxiety are usually at the opposing ends of a vicious cycle. When you lack enough quality sleep, you are bound to feel more stressed, depressed, and anxious. It can be easy to feel overwhelmed when you are tired. You are also likely to have higher levels of irritation, struggle to focus, and just not be in a good mental space. Having a set sleep routine is vital to ensure mental health and happiness.

Nevertheless, stress, anxiety, and other concerns can also be why you aren't getting the sleep your mind and body so desperately need. Anxiety and insomnia can quickly create a negative spiral taking you down emotionally, physically, and mentally. It is why it is so important to be consistent in your sleep patterns and to take all the necessary steps to ensure you get a regular good night's rest.

From all of this, we learn that many factors impact our mindset. It can sometimes be alarming to realize how influenceable our perspectives are. But, it is also good to know that each of these factors impacting our overall mental health also serves as an opportunity to address our concerns.

Perceptions—Always a Concerning Matter

Perceptions refer to the way we witness the world. For us, there may be only one way to see it, and we will defend our perspective with all we have in us. This can be a completely different view for someone else, even when looking at the same thing. Thinking about perceptions helps to keep an image of looking at the world through colored lenses. If you wear red lenses, everything you see will have a red tone. This will be the way you perceive the world. Someone else may be wearing yellow lenses and have a completely different perspective, even though looking at the same things. Often, the color of the lenses we are looking through has a tint of anxiety, changing our entire perspective of our self-image, the world, and what reality looks like.

The Influence of Anxiety on the Perception of Our Action Capabilities

Action capabilities refer to what you think is possible to achieve in life. It refers to how much you think you can achieve. It also determines what challenges you will take, how long you'll persevere when things get hard to complete, and how effectively you overcome obstacles. If the lenses you are looking through at these capabilities are tinted with anxiety, you'll surely have a different idea of what you can achieve than when you rid yourself of this anxiety.

Upon your first exposure to anxiety, you will most likely achieve far more while running on adrenaline and a range of stress hormones. In this scenario, anxiety is good and helps you to achieve much more than without it. Nevertheless, as the human body is not designed to be exposed to stress for long periods, the situation will change soon.

After the initial benefits you may have enjoyed, anxiety will change your perspectives, making you more conservative about what you take on. You may feel less capable of achieving greatness and experience a decline in your self-worth. The hormones that place your body in overdrive turn against its host and wear you down, physically and mentally. This leaves you feeling physically tired, lacking focus, drained, burned out, vulnerable, and depressed.

Anxiety Changes the Way You See the World

It is not only your perceptions of your capabilities that will change but also your perspective on the world.

The law of attraction states that you'll have more of the things you direct your focus on most throughout the day. Anxiety changes your perspectives of the world, driving you to focus on the negative elements of your daily life. It has the power to change your mindset so that the little bit of negativity that forms part of everyday life becomes so magnified, it becomes all you can see. Eventually, it overshadows the good in your life completely.

The only effective way to protect yourself from anxiety's impact on your world perspective is to better understand how our attention works. If your attention is gripped by your lack of money, you will likely experience financial decline as time passes. It is why being grateful can be a helpful tool to overcome this situation. When you express gratitude for all you have, you consciously shift your focus to all you have to gain more of what you want.

Anxiety increases your awareness of the things that make you anxious. There has been a time in history when this could have saved your life. Imagine yourself walking through the jungle, unaware of all the dangers lurking in the thick growth surrounding you. During these times, it was advantageous when anxiety made you aware of the presence of snakes, predators, or spiders that could harm you. Over time, anxiety's purpose has lost its merit, but its impact remains.

In modern times, you are bombarded with things that make you anxious too. You may never have been living in a place where your life is threatened by violence or war. Yet, every time you witness such events on the news, you absorb the same stress and anxiety reflected on the screen. Previously, a car backfiring may just have been a nuisance. Now, the loud sound makes you anxious because your mind has linked the sound to what you've observed in the news. This is how anxiety changes your perspective of the world—it turns what used to be a happy place into one that scares you and limits the life you are living.

How to Separate Facts From Fiction

When you experience anxiety, your body and brain perceive an altered version of the world and reality. This process is called derealization, or creating several illusions in your mind.

These illusions state that you are powerless and in control of the cause of stress and fear in your life. Anxiety lets you believe that you are trapped in the situation and that there is no escape. You can't reach out for help, as you can't trust anyone and everyone is out to get you.

Throughout the book, I will share several techniques on how you can remind yourself, during moments of heightened anxiety, that these images and perceptions are mere figments of the fiction your anxious mind created. While a panic attack lasts no longer than 30 minutes, it can feel extended. There is no need to suffer through it all. There are many ways to break through these images to calm your mind and reclaim an accurate perspective on reality.

Takeaway

When we delve deeper into the origins of the anxious mind, we learn that many contributing factors can place the mind in an anxious state. Before we can free ourselves from the impact of anxiety, we need to explore where it is rooted. This is the only way to effectively rid ourselves of the stronghold an anxious mind can have on our lives.

Chapter Three

How to Improve the Mind

When we are no longer able to change a situation, we are challenged to change ourselves. –Victor Frankl

Most people believe that anxiety is a natural part of life. They think that it's something they just have to deal with and learn to live with. But what if anxiety doesn't have to be a permanent part of your life? What if you could change the way you feel about yourself and break free from the anxiety cycle? It's not easy, but it is possible. You just need to understand how anxiety works and be open to change.

One of the most effective tools for combatting the impact of anxiety is to improve your self-image. Doing so will directly enhance your mindset and reduce the effect of anxiety on your life.

Exploring Happiness

We can place many emotions at the other end of the spectrum, opposing anxiety. For now, I want to focus on happiness as the opposite of anxiety. By doing so, we utilize the law of attraction principle and shift our focus to what we want more in our life. When we explore happiness in detail, we notice specific attributes.

Happiness is a right we all have. We don't have to earn it or even work hard for it; it is just there and accessible to all. Everything in life has the potential to make you happy or anxious. How you will perceive it is entirely up to you.

As the latter is the case, you can train your mind to focus on the good and what is pleasant. Constantly seek the silver lining around the dark clouds; you will gradually cultivate a culture of happiness and gratitude.

Seeking what is good in your life requires consistent mindfulness to shift your focus toward the positive elements in every matter. This does initially require a lot of effort. Still, the rewards are multiple, and the more you invest your focus on finding what is good, the easier it becomes. There is no other known way to find happiness that is more effective than doing this.

The last point I want to make about happiness is probably its most important and widely misunderstood aspect: Nobody can give you happiness or something that transforms your overall state into happiness—happiness is something you find for yourself. This also means that nobody can take away your happiness. People can increase your happiness but can't decide how happy you will be, making this choice entirely up to you.

Seek Clarity to Change Your Self-Image

You need to understand what your self-image should look like before making any changes to it. You also need to understand the purpose and the role of your self-image, as well as how it can support you in the process of overcoming anxiety before you'll be able to make any vital changes to it.

To ensure that your self-image contributes to your state of mind, you need to be sure that it is realistic. It should correspond with the reality of our world and not connect with the possibly distorted perspective you may have of the world.

Someone with a realistic self-image is familiar with their strengths and weaknesses. They know how to use both to their advantage. Even more important, though, is they realize that it is vital to be completely honest with themselves about both concepts. Therefore, you must have a clear understanding of who you are and cease pretending to be someone you are not. You can't go through life with a vague idea of who you are.

Let's visualize the concept for greater clarity. Imagine walking down a staircase you've never been down before, while in the dark. You don't know whether there are turns in the stairs or how far the steps are apart. There is no certainty in your mind, even if all the steps are in place, so you may expect a step to be there, and it is not. This is an anxiety-provoking experience due to the unfamiliarity with your environment. Now imagine walking down the same staircase but this time in bright light. You can see where you are heading, how far the steps are apart, or if there are any possible concerns on your way down. You have a clear image of what you are dealing with and far less stress about the situation. You can confidently progress when you have clarity about who you are along with your strengths and weaknesses. It is why you need to be honest with yourself about every aspect of your being. Even if steps are missing, you can still get down the staircase without injury as you can identify the risk and plan around it.

It is essential to be familiar with exactly who you are and that your self-image perfectly aligns with this reality.

Changing Your Mindset

While you are trapped in the net of anxiety, changing your mindset may appear to be a daunting—or even impossible—task. It doesn't have to be. Let me break down the process into smaller steps, and you'll see there are several ways you can overcome this obstacle effectively.

Imagine a Different Life

Whether you call it imagination or visualization is entirely up to you. Both terms boil down to the same concept—a visual image of the future, circumstances, possible events, or challenges ahead.

Initially, it may be easy to make these images out to be nothing but mere fantasies. That said, these "fantasies" play a vital role in our behavior. It is only natural to adjust how we present ourselves and our actions according to the images we have in our minds about a specific situation or even a person. If you imagine that someone doesn't like you, you may prefer to avoid that person, whereas if you visualized the two of you becoming best friends, you would come across as warm, welcoming, and friendly. In both scenarios, the person is still the same; it merely was what you imagined about that person that changed.

The power of our imagination goes underestimated. We fail to see how much it impacts our lives and shapes our choices and actions. Once you realize the value of imagination in your life, you can utilize it to change your personality, self-image, and mindset. The visual images we host enable us to shape our reality by imagining the life we desire. We can have practice runs in our minds of how matters will play out and how we will actively change our lives. You can become that person in your mind before you become empowered, confident, or optimistic in real life. It can also happen with far less effort—you just need to direct your thoughts the way you want them to go.

The secret to these visualizations is that the human mind struggles to distinguish between reality and vivid visualizations. Thus, if you imagine a life you desire and color in as many details as possible, you are actively creating the blueprint for your life. Of course, this also highlights why imagination is a major contributing factor to anxiety. Suppose you allow your mind to constantly visualize the worst to happen. If so, you are actively creating that life, leaving you feeling anxious.

Wipe Out Any False Beliefs

What are the false beliefs you hold onto in life? Can you identify the beliefs you treasure without any proof or facts?

When you manifested these beliefs, there was no effort involved, so it happened organically. You didn't have to force yourself to believe these things—it just happened. Habits form in much the same manner. You did something once, twice, maybe three times, and then it became a habit without effort.

The same approach can serve you well when you want to shed these beliefs and replace them with positive alternatives. Before you can achieve this, learning how to relax is a must. You need to make an effort to become calm and tranquil. There are several ways you can seek deeper relaxation; some examples are meditating, taking a walk in nature, or simply playing with your pets. You'll know better, though, what actions help you to reach a deeper state of relaxation. Once you've immersed yourself in physical relaxation, you'll gradually shift into a state of mental relaxation and serenity. In this state, you can fully explore the beliefs you cherish and set yourself free from the false beliefs you have.

The best way to shed a false belief is to ask questions to test its validity. By asking and answering questions related to the belief, you will soon see that it is a false belief.

Embrace a Growth Mindset

Early on, I explained the differences between a fixed and a growth mindset. A growth mindset combats stress and anxiety, as it sees opportunities rather than obstacles. It is also necessary if you want to enjoy personal and professional success and set yourself apart from the rest. When you approach life with a growth mindset, you recognize fear as a feeling that can hold you back or propel you forward—you choose the latter.

The following steps can help you to manifest this change:

- Identify the triggers causing you to levitate towards a fixed mindset. The endless options here can be anything from a specific behavior to certain places, people, or even circumstances.

- Be more mindful and become aware of the internal chatter occupying your mind. What is the voice of doubt and fear whispering in your ear?

- Recognize the fear in which the voice of the fixed mindset is rooted. Identify what you are scared of and what is holding you back. Is it perhaps the feeling of rejection, being lonely, failing, or even public humiliation?

- The more you try to push this fear away, the stronger its presence will become; instead, embrace your fears. The old saying goes that we must keep our friends close and our enemies closer. As a reflection of that idea, you want to keep your fears close, for then it is easy to recognize them as nothing but emotion. The more time you spend with your fear, the less scary it becomes until it is completely gone.

- Your big breakthrough will come when you realize that you have a choice in which mindset you choose. You always have a choice in whether you will see obstacles or opportunities. While you may not always be successful with the opportunities you've identified, your approach to the matter will be vastly different.

- This is when you recognize the fixed mindset for what it is and how it keeps you back in life. Now is the time to replace this with a growth mindset.

Throughout the process, make sure you remain flexible. Being on the path of the least resistance demands that we can change and adapt quickly. As you are now employing the growth mindset, practice different approaches to being more fluid in your choices and actions.

Instill a Happiness Habit

Get used to being happy. If you've been unhappy for so long, you may initially feel uncomfortable when you have your first taste of happiness. It can be that you've sought after this for so long that you struggle to accept it in your life. It can even be that you consider happiness more complex than it truly is. Happiness is nothing but a state of mind in which you perceive matters to be favorable and pleasant. It is not a gift that anyone gave you; rather, it is merely a choice you've made for yourself.

Replace the Influx of Negativity With Positive Information

Identify the sources of negativity in your life. Perhaps it is the people you surround yourself with, the activities you partake in, or even the content you regularly consume. Once you can distinguish which of these sources are positive and negative, you can remove the negative ones from your life and replace them with positive ones.

Choose to Be Successful

You can be successful in your mind long before you make it into a reality. By visualizing your success, you'll determine what success means to you, how you'll know you are successful, and what your life will be like when you are successful. What will you wear, eat, and say when you are successful? Start doing these things even before you are successful, and success will naturally follow too.

The following are all features of a successful personality. Begin by incorporating these goals into your life:

- You know where you are heading in life.

- It is easy to show compassion towards others without neglecting your needs.

- You may be scared, but have the courage to face your fears.

- Life is easier as you have a greater understanding of its elements.

- You are confident in your capabilities.

- You love and accept yourself for who you are.

- You show esteem for everything you have.

Understanding the Anxiety Cycle

What is the pattern of your anxiety? As anxiety can be a habit, you can repeat the same habit loops when it comes to your anxiety cycle. To identify these loops, you need to identify your triggers, cues, routines, and rewards. This is possible when you employ greater awareness of how your anxiety manifests. A helpful aid in this regard is journaling your experiences and the accompanying emotions. This will help you create a record of your experiences and identify your anxiety cycle. It is necessary if you want to break free from the loop you are trapped in. You can address these concerns effectively once you employ greater awareness of what you feel and experience.

Before you can change your thoughts and get rid of your anxiety, you need to understand how the human mind works and how you employ habits to your benefit. The anxiety cycle or habit loop centered around anxiety starts with a cue or trigger that prompts neurons in the brain to fire and cause a routine or reaction. Afterward, there is always a reward. Many things can serve as triggers, instigating action by triggering the brain into a specific chain of reactions through one of our senses.

A routine is an action that is required as a response to the trigger. Often, this would require physical activity or even thoughts that cause increased anxiety levels. The reward is what encourages you to repeat the same loop again.

The Anxiety Habit Loop

When you wake up in the morning, you brush your teeth, have your first cup of coffee, or follow any other ritual you are familiar with. You don't think about these actions any longer as they are habits. Through habits, you reduce the pressure on your mind by minimizing the choices you need to think about. You can employ the same ability to create habits that automatically remove specific thoughts to prevent them from being negative. We will be exploring habits in much greater depth later on. For now, I just want to touch on how you can use habits to reduce anxiety.

Rewards play a crucial role when you are forming new habits. They can take on several forms; for example, when something has triggered your mind to worry, the fact that you are worrying often serves as the reward. Worrying can leave you feeling like you've done something about the concern while, in essence, you didn't do anything productively. Yet, worrying feels like you've taken action and didn't just leave it, and this is your reward, encouraging you to repeat the same loop again.

Habit loops can be highly beneficial and free up the brain's capacity to focus on more vital things. However, when these habit loops are formed under stressful or undesired circumstances, the neurons can fire in all directions, causing poor habit loops to form. Say you were a victim of an armed robbery and the fear you felt was triggered by a convenience store gunman—your mind immediately shifted into the fight-or-flight response, leaving you feeling paralyzed. During the entire ordeal, you were even unable to move. Since the tragedy, you experience the same reaction whenever you go to a convenience store. It means that the convenience store has become a trigger of a negative habit loop. Consequently, habit loops require and emphasize great care and clarity when being formed.

You must be clear on what you want to achieve when actively working on your habits to change them to your benefit. Before making any changes, draft a plan of what you want to achieve, and only then start working on changing your habits. This will give your approach structure and direction, ensuring success.

As the anxiety cycle consists of a habit loop, you need to replace the habit loop with one that is positive. When serious about making such changes, you must be willing to repeat the same cycles. Repetition is the most effective way to set new habits in place. Remain consistent in your effort, and while you are making these changes, try to have fun; finding something to enjoy can alleviate the challenging, difficult aspects of this transition.

With changes to your behaviors and habits come physical changes to your brain. Neuroplasticity refers to the brain's ability to change itself, which plays a crucial role in forming and changing these loops. It allows for new pathways to form, and it is how you can actively change the physical structure of your brain. Through this change, you can change your responses to various triggers and events to allow different emotions to present themselves and replace your stress and anxiety.

When you are more mindful and aware of your thoughts, you can quickly recognize which thoughts are helpful and which are merely causing anxiety. Approach these thoughts with a curiosity to explore whether they are grounded in reality in any way. This way, you can clear your mind of thoughts that don't benefit your mindset and mental health. Once you get rid of these negative thoughts, replace them with positive ones.

Old Habits Can Be Hard to Break

Change is often underestimated for how hard it is to achieve. Changing our habits is even harder to do, as our brains are running on autopilot when habits keep us busy. Each part of the brain has different functions. The prefrontal cortex is primarily used for more complex tasks like active thinking and decision-making, meaning it requires a lot of energy. It is also the part of the brain we depend on to create new habits, so creating new habits demands a lot of energy. At the same time, habitual actions don't rely on this part of the brain and can slip past with minimum effort.

Activities That Improve the Mind

Using the mind-body connection, you can create, change, and improve your mind through physical activities and actions.

Yoga and Meditation

Both these ancient practices have been used for ages to still the mind. It encourages the ability to focus your thoughts on only one thought and to silence the many other thoughts that are constantly rushing through your mind. When you gain greater control over your thoughts, you can employ greater awareness of what thoughts you have. This will help you to effectively manage them.

Fasting

Through fasting, you will increase your perseverance and increase your willpower. Fasting demands that your commitment to long-term goals enjoy favor over instant gratification. Enhancing this ability will improve the way you take control of your thoughts to help you enjoy a healthier mindset.

Mindfulness

You will no longer tolerate negative self-talk or allow negative thoughts to drag you down through increased awareness. Mindfulness is a learned behavior; you can become more mindful by becoming aware of the sensations you enjoy during your day. When you bathe or shower, take a moment to notice the sensation of the hot water on your skin; or, when you eat, notice your food's taste and texture. It can be easy to get so caught up in deadlines and the stress of your responsibilities that many of these things slip you by. Mindfulness teaches you to stop and experience life in its fullness.

Positive Visualization

I've mentioned that the mind struggles to distinguish between imagination and reality. Use this to your benefit by visualizing the life you desire, and gradually, your life will turn in this direction.

Identifying and Practicing Your Passions

It is common to feel exhausted after spending several hours doing something you don't like or find boring. In contrast, you can spend equal time doing something you're passionate about and feel completely different. Spending time with your passions leaves you motivated to do even more. This happens because our passions excite us. If you haven't identified your passions yet, think about the things you like doing to determine whether these are passions of yours. Once you've identified your passions, spend time doing them, as they are a natural way to boost your mindset.

Other Techniques to Instill Change in the Subconscious Mind

There are other techniques you can use to change the way your subconscious mind works:

- Affirmations: Make positive statements about yourself, preferably in front of a mirror, to gradually change how you perceive yourself.

- Surround yourself with positivity: Emotions are nothing but energy waves. The type of waves you surround yourself with impact your internal energy waves. Suppose you surround yourself with negative energy waves. By doing so, you are bound to become more negative, and the same is true when you surround yourself with positive people.

- Visualize success: Make time daily to visualize how your life changes when you achieve your goals and enjoy the success you desire.

- Listen to binaural beats: The neurons in our brains work on electric impulses. By listening to these beats, you can manipulate these neurons to enjoy your desired mental state.

- Hypnosis: Similar to binaural beats, hypnosis can also manipulate your brain function and change the state of your mindset.

These techniques are all proven to be highly successful. In the next chapter, I explore a somewhat different approach to an improved and sustained mental wellness through the support of the gut. By taking care of your gut health and providing the body with the nutrition it needs, you can create a significant improvement in your mental health.

Takeaway

Being happy, positive, content, and relaxed is a choice we have to make daily. Sometimes, maintaining a positive state can be very challenging. This chapter explored several ways to improve your state of mind and discussed techniques to help you strengthen your positive mindset. These techniques will also help you to let go of negative habits that make it harder to maintain a state of positivity.

Chapter Four

How to Improve Your Gut Health

The road to health is paved with good intestines!
–Sherry A. Rogers

For ages, we've been expressing our emotions as we experience them in our gut. We say that we feel butterflies in our stomachs or have a gut feeling. Sometimes, we say that our intestines are in a knot or a twist. Further, it was far more recently that we started to connect the dots between our intestines' health and mental state. Now, we know that the two systems are undeniably linked. While your mindset impacts your gut and the sensations you experience here, the gut is as much of a role player, contributing to your state of mind.

One way the brain impacts the stomach is that merely the thought of food and eating is enough indication to your stomach to release digestive fluids. It means the visualization of food or imagining eating impacts the body physically. It is also evident in many other medical concerns linked to your emotional state; just think about indigestion, heartburn, and abdominal cramps caused by high-stress situations.

We need to explore the connection and the science behind these two systems to learn how we can address mindset challenges by improving our gut health.

Microbiome

The best place to start is always by exploring the most basic parts of the system. For the digestive system, this would be with the microbiome.

What Is a Microbiome?

Microbiome is a term used to refer to a collection or community of microorganisms living in a specific environment. These types of microorganisms include bacteria, fungi, or viruses, and these particular communities of microorganisms can be found in several areas of the human body. Some of the places where you'll find them are on your skin and also in the gut area. We have long believed that all microorganisms are bad and harmful to the body. Thanks to modern science and the technology available to explore these microorganisms, we know they fulfill a vital function of sustaining health and well-being. Yes, there are harmful pathogens, but to a large extent, the microbiome takes up most of the space to prevent pathogens from finding a place in these systems while contributing to a range of bodily functions necessary to sustain your health. In the gut, the microbiome helps digestion and break down food.

As they are vital to our well-being, we need to consider the factors that can impact the state of these systems. In the gut, some of the most common factors affecting these systems are diet, medicine, and exercise.

Exploring the Gut-Brain Axis

The gut-brain axis (GBA) is a communication system linking the central and enteric nervous systems. In other words, the system enables the brain and the gut to communicate. In this equation, the brain remains the organ, allowing the mind to process thoughts, experiences, and emotions. It is how the state of the gut impacts the state of mind you are in.

The communication between the gut and the brain is a bidirectional communication network, meaning the gut can send messages to the brain and vice versa. The system consists of millions of neurons that communicate with each other through a range of pathways. In the gut, the microbiome is the source of the message sent to the brain. There are roughly 100 million neurons in the brain—the gut area exceeds this number by far, as it has an estimated 500 million neurons communicating with the brain (Robertson, 2020). This number of neurons is similar to what can be found in the spine, all of which are linked via the nervous system. The vagus nerve is one of the most profound nerves, connecting all these neurons to enable effective communication.

The impact of what we sense in the gut area can influence many areas of our existence. It will affect certain everyday choices, like what food and drinks you would consume. But it goes much deeper than that, as it also determines whose company we prefer and how we perceive and process information. As such, the state of our gut health can have an effect on our well-being that goes beyond the physical sense.

One interesting link between the gut and your state of mind is the connection between gut bacteria and depression. During the state of depression, activity in the intestine slows to an almost complete standstill. At the same time, the gut microbiota is widely considered the second most significant contributing factor to depression across the US (Ghannoum et al., 2021). We just can't deny the impact that the state of your gut health has on complex communication and interaction between your mind and your emotional wellness.

This impact is to such an extent that medical professionals can diagnose and classify depression patients merely by considering their gut microbiota. In fact, researchers have transferred microbiome bacteria from a healthy person to a depressed person; after the transfer, the depression symptoms were immediately relieved (Ghannoum et al., 2021).

When we change the state of the gut bacteria, it has a direct impact on the state of the brain. One of the critical role players in establishing such improvement is probiotics. Probiotics are good gut bacteria, but they aren't all the same. Some different types of probiotics affect other areas of the body. Probiotics that are specifically linked to the brain are often called "psychobiotics". These live bacteria can improve depression, anxiety, and stress symptoms.

Studies also reveal that probiotics aid mental health by making the brain less responsive to various emotional triggers, such as anger, sorrow, and fear. Through the same studies, scientists also discovered that probiotics lower the emotional response to stimuli that can cause an increase in negative emotions. This leads us to the latest studies presenting preliminary results indicating that probiotics can serve as a medium to relieve the symptoms of depression (Mayer, 2018). Similar to probiotics, another other key player is prebiotics. When fibers get fermented by the bacteria in the gut, you get prebiotics. They are also linked to improving brain health as they can reduce cortisol levels, the stress hormone (Robertson, 2020). Together, these organisms demonstrate the delicate, strong connection between the gut and mind.

The Gut Stores Serotonin

Serotonin is a happy hormone. When our serotonin levels drop too low, depression symptoms start to show. Therefore, protecting our production and storage of this vital hormone is vital.

The intestine is the largest storage facility of serotonin; up to 95% of the body's serotonin can be found in the gut (Mayer, 2018). Some of the roles this hormone fulfills are to aid the digestive system as well as serving as a signaling molecule in GBA. Serotonin also regulates sleep patterns, controlling pain sensitivity, managing appetite, mood, and holistic health (Mayer, 2018). Recent research has also found that microbes in the gut stimulate the production of serotonin in the body. It is just another way the gut can significantly impact overall mental health and wellness.

The impact of gut health on the mind is also bidirectional. The better your mind's state, the better your gut's state, and vice versa. Relaxing your mind, lowering your stressors, being more mindful of the thoughts you host, and stopping the ruminating mind from pondering on negativity will directly impact the gut microbe composition. Furthermore, you can also keep your gut health in mint condition through the food you eat. But what is the right food to eat to keep the microbes in your gut happy?

Keeping the Gut Healthy Through Nutrition

It can be so easy to fall into the trap of mindless eating. Sometimes, we eat without even considering what we put into our mouths and systems. The reality is that whatever we eat will pass through our digestive system and feed either the good bacteria—and help them to stay healthy and in great numbers—or the bad bacteria—having the same effect on them. For many, this realization is a much-needed wake-up call to be more discerning about what they consume and how they do so.

Changing your diet will most likely not bring about an immediate and rapid improvement in your depression symptoms or your high level of anxiety. However, when you combine a healthy diet with exercise and shift your mindset positively, you will notice a significant improvement in your mood over time. Not only will your mood and mental health benefit from these changes, but making these changes will also boost your immune system and your serotonin levels.

It may be helpful to think of your gut the same way you regard the flower beds in your garden. Just like the flowers in these beds will flourish if you clear the weeds, do regular composting, and keep them free from pests and unwanted insects, your entire system will flourish when you take proper care of your gut.

The Impact Your Eating Habits Have on Your Gut Health

When we focus on the interior of the gut, we'll find a living and changing ecosystem. Like any other ecosystem, this one is also constantly evolving. External factors influence the state of the ecosystem and determine whether the organisms forming part of these systems are growing, increasing, dying, sick, or in any other state in between. The external factors include our lifestyle, diet, stress levels, activity level, and overall health and wellness.

When this ecosystem is in an optimal state, it also contributes to having a healthy host, as gut health also impacts our immune system. Today, one of the most significant concerns in the medical field is the immense lack of healthy eating habits in modern society. The widely promoted, preferred, and consumed foods do not sustain a healthy gut environment. It is often harmful to the sensitive ecosystem inside our intestines, causing our eating to immensely negatively impact our overall health and wellness.

Exploring Gut Microbiota, the Intestinal Barrier, and the Immune System

We need to understand the impact various components and dietary habits have on our gut health before we can make any valuable nutritional changes. Inside the gastrointestinal tract is a multi-layered ecosystem between the microbiota and the host, your intestine. The intestinal barrier is where nutrient uptake takes place. Therefore, it needs to be in optimal condition to ensure the body has access to all the necessary nutrients to survive and thrive. It is also where the body clears itself from unwanted macromolecules potentially dangerous to the entire system. The whole system is extremely complex and highly sensitive to external factors, of which diet is one. If the system is not in an optimal state, it can, of course, lead to various physical and mental health concerns.

Carbohydrates and Gut Microbiota

We can divide carbohydrates into two categories: digestible and indigestible. Digestible carbohydrates include a range of sugars like fructose, glucose, and galactose. These are all degraded in the small intestine and then released into the bloodstream as glucose energy. Indigestible carbohydrates, on the other hand, mostly consist of fiber and are hard to digest. These pass through the entire digestive system to the large intestine. Examples of these carbohydrates are resistant starch and fiber in fruit, vegetables, and whole grains.

Indigestible carbohydrates can be further divided into fermentable and nonfermentable, referring to whether it will ferment in the colon or not. Fiber can also be categorized as soluble or insoluble in water. Fiber that is nonfermentable and insoluble passes through the digestive tract and aids in preventing constipation by softening the stool.

When fermentable fiber goes through the fermentation process, it yields short-chain fatty acids (SCFAs). While certain parts of SCFAs take care of cholesterol metabolism, others play an essential role in caring for the tissue barrier of the intestine. As it is also involved in the absorption of water and salt, it aids in the mucus health inside the digestive tract.

Prebiotics are non-digestible fibers that promote the growth and activity of beneficial gut bacteria, which then produce short-chain fatty acids (SCFAs) during metabolism. The intestinal mucus tract degrades when the diet contains insufficient prebiotics. Prebiotics are like "food" for good bacteria and can keep your gut and digestive system healthy, and they can strengthen your gut health by increasing "good" bacteria (Rinninella et al., 2019).

Proteins and Gut Microbiota

Proteins consist of animal protein and plant-based protein. During the fermentation of animal protein, especially red meat, the substances released into the intestine support bacteria growth, increasing other compounds that contribute to heart disease (Rinninella et al., 2019).

Furthermore, research indicates that the body digests proteins and breaks them down into amino acids (Meg, 2022). These amino acids play a vital role in the production of neurotransmitters, making them an essential piece to a healthy diet for our brains.

By including poultry, dairy, nuts, and fish in your diet, you increase the quantity of L-tryptophan, the specific amino acid that acts as a serotonin precursor (Meg, 2022). In conjunction, there is also a link between low tryptophan and dietary protein levels and anxiety. This anxious state is worsened even further by a high-fat diet; high intake of refined carbohydrates and sugar; and other unhealthy eating habits (Meg, 2022).

To counteract the effects of a high-carbohydrate diet, substitute dietary choices with protein. During fermentation, plant-based protein decreases the harmful bacteria in the gut and increases bacteria contributing to overall gut health (Rinninella et al., 2019).

Fats and Gut Microbiota

The amount and type of fat you consume will influence fat consumption's impact on the intestine. There are three fat categories: saturated, monounsaturated, and polyunsaturated. Food products derived from mammals are usually high in saturated fats. Research shows that a high intake of these fats can lead to an imbalance in bacteria in the intestine (Rinninella et al., 2019). Other studies also indicate a link between high-fat intake and increased anxiety (Dutheil et al., 2015).

This doesn't mean you have to avoid fat entirely; opt for foods high in other fats, like monounsaturated fat. The most widely available monounsaturated fat is olive oil, which helps to reduce the risk of heart disease and is one of the critical ingredients of the Mediterranean diet (Rinninella et al., 2019).

Another healthy fat substitute is polyunsaturated fats; they include sunflower and corn oil, seeds, and nuts. These oils are essential fatty acids as the body can't generate these internally and depend on a diet that includes the necessary oil. This specific oil is closely linked to lowering inflammation in the body and the intestine (Rinninella et al., 2019).

Salt and Gut Microbiota

Excessive salt intake raises blood pressure and increases the heart's workload, causing the body to release adrenaline into the bloodstream and leading to anxiety. It also increases the risk of developing gastric cancers as it damages the mucus in the gastric tract (Rinninella et al., 2019).

Food Additives and Gut Microbiota

Preservatives, flavorings, and colorants are all ingredients you'll find on the labels of processed foods. These ingredients hold the potential to change the entire internal landscape of the gastrointestinal tract. Not only that, they also limit the diversity of the good bacteria in the intestine (Rinninella et al., 2019).

During a study conducted by Georgia State researchers, they determined that dietary emulsifiers—the food additives found in most processed foods—can also have an adverse impact on your mindset. These additives are used to improve the texture and extend the shelf life of these food products, but these studies showed that they have a negative impact by increasing anxiety-related and social behaviors in mice (Holder et al., 2019).

Micronutrients and Gut Microbiota

Vitamins and minerals fall under the micronutrient category. They are both beneficial in sustaining the gut's health and play a significant role in increasing the number of good bacteria and supporting their growth.

Over recent years, research studies explored the role of micronutrients in sustaining a healthy gut as a way to ease the symptoms of anxiety and depression. Their findings emphasized the important role micronutrients have to play: The participants showed a dramatic improvement after taking a blend of 40 ingredients that included botanicals, minerals, amino acids, and vitamins. These findings align with more than 100 previous studies confirming the role broad-spectrum micronutrients play in sustaining excellent mental health and relieving mood concerns ("Micronutrients as a Treatment," 2018).

Here, I would like to highlight vitamin D as it is a known micronutrient that holds the potential to change the composition of gut bacteria (Rinninella et al., 2019).

Polyphenols and Gut Microbiota

Polyphenols are present in a vast range of plants and foods. The impact of polyphenols on the gut is still under research; however, there appears to be a strong link between polyphenols and gut microbiota (Rinninella et al., 2019).

The role of polyphenols in treating anxiety and depression was further established by a recent study that explored and confirmed the role polyphenols have to play in improving the symptoms of both conditions (Lin et al., 2021).

Various Popular Dietary Habits and Microbiota

Vegan and Vegetarian Diets

As vegan diets consist of only plant-based foods, it is a wonderful way to increase the number and diversity of gut microbiota in the intestine.

Gluten-Free Diet

For many people, following a gluten-free diet is not a choice but a necessity to improve their health. You can improve the state of your gut and reduce inflammation caused by your body's intolerance towards gluten when opting for a gluten-free diet, as is the case with celiac disease. Still, even though you can't reverse all the damage caused by gluten, going gluten-free will be helpful for improving the state of your gut microbiota.

Ketogenic Diet

Given the keto diet is so high in protein and contains very little fiber, it can harm the microbiota and increase inflammation in the intestine.

High-Glucose and High-Fructose Diets

The impact of these diet choices can become a significant concern over time. Content that is high in fructose or glucose can alter the composition of microbiota in the gut. This type of diet can also lead to obesity.

Low-FODMAP Diet

A diet low in fermentable oligosaccharides, disaccharides, monosaccharides and polyols (FODMAP) can reduce inflammation in the intestine of those who suffer from intestinal bacterial overgrowth and irritable bowel syndrome (IBS). However, it also reduces the plant material the microbiota needs to sustain itself. Thus, this is not a recommended choice over extended periods.

Western Diet

The Western diet is high in fat and sugar, and it contains a lot of processed foods. These are like poison to the gut microbiota and can increase inflammation and even cause inflammatory bowel syndrome.

Mediterranean Diet

The Mediterranean diet is known for its many health benefits. The food included in this diet type aids in reducing inflammation and supporting good gut bacteria. It is also an excellent way to support the gut bacteria that supports aging.

Vegan and Vegetarian Diet	Gluten-Free Diet	Ketogenic Diet	Low FODMAP Diet	Western Diet	Mediterranean Diet
Unclear role on biodiversity	**Decrease** of healthy bacteria abundance	**Decrease** of bacteria abundance and diversity	**Decrease** of total bacteria abundance	**Decrease** of total microbiota diversity	**Augmentation** of microbiota diversity and stability

The Impact of Diets on Gut Health

Foods That Are Harmful to the Gut Environment

I want to stress that foods harmful to your gut should be consumed in moderation. But, I know it is often the case that limiting your intake of these foods can be challenging. Knowing exactly how much of these foods is still acceptable to consume can also be tricky. Therefore, complete abstinence may be the best way to go if you want to be sure you are on the safe side. The best way to approach these foods would be to see what changes your lifestyle and budget allow you to limit or avoid any of these foods.

- processed food: includes processed meat products

- refined sugars: these are present in all fast-food options, fine pastries, pasta, and all food made with white flour, like pizza bases

- artificial sweeteners

- food with antibiotics: most commercially-farmed meat contains antibiotics

- caffeine

- alcohol

Food That Feeds the Soul—And the Gut

The following are all foods you can have plenty of as they contribute to the overall state of the gut by caring for the microbiomes:

- water: rinses the system and clears it of toxins

- good fuel: food types naturally high in energy, like avocados and coconuts

- good quality fat: examples include olive and fish oils

- functional carbohydrate: whole grains and unrefined products

- non-energy nutrients: foods high in minerals, vitamins, and fiber, like most vegetables

- vitamins: most fruit and vegetables are high in vitamins

- minerals: mostly present in raw fruit and vegetables

- herbs: if fresh, can have many medicinal properties that contribute to overall health

- functional mushrooms: specific mushrooms that hold a vast number of health benefits, like shitake, reishi, and oyster mushrooms

- prebiotics and probiotics: can be taken as supplements

but are also present in many food options

- fermented food: examples are kefir, sauerkraut, and yogurt

It becomes easier to make good and healthy choices regarding what you eat when you understand the impact these different food types have on your health. While you can take a more direct approach toward your diet, sticking to the foods listed above, and avoiding or minimizing your intake of the foods that are bad for your gut health, will already bring about a range of physical and mental health benefits.

Takeaway

We can no longer deny the link between the gut and the brain. The chemicals in our body serve as a direct communication channel, allowing both systems to impact each other positively or negatively. As a result, the state of your gut influences the state of your mind. By making healthy choices, including foods that contribute to gut health, staying hydrated, and excluding unhealthy food options, you can create a healthier environment in your gut to sustain good gut bacteria and mental well-being.

Chapter Five

Mind-Body Connection

Life is hard. Life is difficult. Life is going to punch you in the gut. But when you change your attitude, you change your behavior. When your behavior changes, so do your results. –Will Hurd

Sandy has been burning the candle at both ends for the past couple of weeks. She has been working immensely long hours without taking a single day off. Sandy is busy building her business while working for a company too. However, Sandy doesn't mind working so hard; she knows what she wants for her life and is adamant about getting it.

Nevertheless, one morning Sandy woke up and felt completely drained. She thought that her business was nothing but a pipe dream. As she became so discouraged, she ceased working at all on her vision for several days. It now feels like she is stuck in her life and will never escape. She thinks she was silly to even try to create a new life for herself.

Sandy is not a unique case. We have witnessed Sandy's life over the past couple of weeks that she burned herself out physically, and this exhaustion is now affecting her mental state. Sandy is a clear example of how the mind-body connection works.

In simple terms, we can say that the mind-body connection refers to the effect our feelings have on our physical health and how our physical state affects how we feel and perceive the world. Yet, it is a concept demanding much deeper digging to truly understand how it works so that you can employ the connection to your benefit.

What Is the Mind-Body Connection?

This is one of those concepts that yield a significant lack of consensus. Experts in various professional fields disagree implicitly and explicitly about what it entails. Finding any agreement regarding how the connection is perceived can be challenging, even in literature.

In a way, the argument that mind and body are merely two labels referring to different parts of the same system makes a lot of sense. Both parts contribute to the human body's effective functioning and influence each other. Once we consider the relationship between mind and body and take a holistic approach to well-being, it becomes evident that this bond holds several implications in the theory and practice of psychotherapy.

> Dr. James Gordon, the Center for Mind-Body Medicine founder, explains this relationship: "The brain and the peripheral nervous system, the endocrine and immune systems, and indeed, all the organs of our body and all the emotional responses we have, share a common chemical language and are constantly communicating with one another" (Hart, n.d., para. 8).

Often without us ever being aware of what is taking place internally, a lot of communication occurs behind the scenes as various parts of our bodies communicate. I can't overemphasize the importance of this chemical language that serves as the communication medium. We rely on this when we want to address various mental concerns by incorporating transformation on the physical side of our being.

How Does the Mind-Body Connection Work?

Now that you have a basic understanding of this connection, we can continue exploring how it works. When we have a thorough grasp of the processes that are essentially at the core of the connection, we can utilize them in our favor. It is how we can effectively address mental health concerns through activities like exercise, yoga, and more which we'll explore soon.

The mind-body connection consists of a feedback loop between mind and body in its most basic form. It means that what we think impacts how we feel, and how we feel influences how we think. Take Sandy for instance: When she was energized, she was excited and optimistic about her business. Once she felt tired, her thoughts about the future of her business took a downward turn, and she struggled to see any bright future.

The concept of feeling is often misunderstood. Many would say that when they feel certain emotions like excitement, sadness, anger, or any other, the process of feeling occurs in the mind. That is not the case—feeling has to do with a physical response or experience. When you are feeling excitement, it is due to the physical sensations you experience in your body, creating an awareness of what you are feeling. Feeling is always a bodily experience.

Let's say you are feeling nervous. The sensation making you aware of nervousness didn't originate in your mind. No, the mind communicates by employing this chemical language to the body to increase your heart rate, change your posture, and even elevate your blood pressure. As being nervous indicates that the body isn't in a state of rest optimal for digestion, there are specific changes in your digestive system too. As you become aware of these sensations in your body and recognize them as being linked to feeling nervous, you can identify what you are feeling. The same goes for every other emotion you are feeling.

When you feel confident, it is because your body is standing upright; you are calm and relaxed; and your heart rate is at a reasonable pace. You may experience no discomfort in your body at all. Being anxious, depressed, or stressed are all emotions you become aware of when your body transitions into a state, making you aware of what you are feeling. Suddenly, the term feeling makes a lot more sense, doesn't it?

Your feelings influence how you think, but we've mentioned that the communication between your mind and body is a dialogue. So, what you think also impacts what you feel. What are the thoughts you think when you are feeling anxious? Maybe, like Sandy, you think you are trapped in a life you don't like much. You don't have to ponder on such thoughts for long before your body begins to change, making you aware of the sensations accompanying this way of thinking.

Still not convinced? Why not test this phenomenon for yourself? When you are in a relaxed state of mind, shift your focus to thoughts you know usually leave you feeling anxious. Do so for a couple of minutes and see if you can perceive any physical changes in your body. Maybe you feel a little less relaxed, and a muscle spasm is tightening up in your neck and shoulders. Perhaps you can feel your gut beginning to feel weird, as if your intestines are in a twist. These feelings you are experiencing are the results of the physical changes your mind has communicated to your body through their chemical language.

I don't want to leave you in a stressed-out state, so, please, reverse the effect by shifting your focus to things that make you feel relaxed and at peace. Now, you've experienced how effective this communication platform between mind and body is.

How can you make this work for you? Next time you are feeling stressed out, try to change your posture. Stand up straight and pull back your shoulders. Opening up your chest cavity gives your lungs space to breathe a little deeper, relieving the pressure you may experience in your chest. When you feel like crying, instead of dropping your head to hide your tears, raise your eyes to the sky above. It is physically impossible for the body to shed tears when you have an upwards gaze. The added benefit is that it will immediately lift your mood and prevent the tears, which many find humiliating. Changing your posture whenever you feel tired, overwhelmed, anxious, depressed, stressed, or any other uncomfortable emotions dragging you down. The next time you feel this way, make a conscious effort to lift your head, pull back your shoulders, stand confidently, and breathe deeply; it will do wonders for your mood.

Never underestimate the change you can bring about in your overall state simply by changing how you breathe. It is the simplest thing to do and has an immense impact on how you feel. When your mind releases a surge of stress hormones, your body responds with a rapid heart rate and increased blood pressure. Blood is drawn away from your digestive system to carry oxygen to your muscles. Your breathing becomes shallow and fast to support all these physical changes. Your body's response results from the communication sent from your brain to the body utilizing the existing chemical language. When you want the opposite effect, you must use your body to communicate to your brain that there is no threat and that it can lower the secretion of stress hormones. By taking deep and slow breaths, you are instigating this change and are telling your brain to chill out. The chain reaction to slowing your breathing includes slowing your heart rate, lowering your blood pressure, and allowing your body to return to a state of calm, directing your brain to do the same.

Just as there are specific actions you can take to instantly improve your state, there are also other valuable activities you can include in your daily routine to enjoy long-term relief from anxiety, stress, and even depression.

Exercise as an Aid to Alleviate Anxiety

Feeling anxious? A brisk walk of only 10 minutes can immediately relieve the symptoms you are experiencing. Knowing that you can enjoy the same immediate relief from anxiety symptoms from going for a 2-mile jog or a 10-minute brisk walk is essential. While this relief may not last as long as when you regularly exercise, you will still be able to improve the way your body feels and, as a result, the state of your mind.

When you exercise, you engage your mind in something other than the stress-provoking thoughts that have been consuming and keeping you in this state. While moving about, you loosen your muscles and increase circulation. By lessening the amount of tension you are feeling, your body communicates to the brain to change its state too.

Exercise also increases your heart rate, which directly triggers the brain to release a different batch of chemicals. Part of the series of actions you instigate simply by being active is that you wake up the frontal regions of the brain. This brain region is responsible for executive functioning and can overrule the activity in the amygdala. The amygdala is located at the bottom of the brain and is what you depend on for survival. However, the amygdala is incapable of logical thinking and merely reacts to external stimuli. Such is the case when you are anxious—you are mentally trapped in a fight-or-flight state. When activating the frontal region, your conscious mind and logical thinking take over. It is how you get out of this state by realizing you are facing no immediate threat.

Regular exercising and making it part of your daily routine increases your internal resources to face the storms of life with greater resilience. It is how you can enjoy long-term benefits from exercising. You are using your body to feel differently, communicating to your brain to think differently.

Still today, research is still inconclusive regarding how much you need to exercise or how strenuous it should be. But, experts state that patients with an anxiety disorder who are involved in high-level physical activity show faster improvement of their symptoms and are more protected against the impact of these symptoms (Ratey, 2019).

When it comes to including regular exercise into your daily routine as part of your anxiety treatment, two points are vital to remember:

1. The more you do, the better it is.

2. Just start and see where it takes you; progress is better than perfection.

It can be challenging to start with an exercise regime if you haven't been exercising. The symptoms you are experiencing can make it even more challenging to start. The following tips can help you to get going:

- Commit yourself to only 30 minutes of exercising 5 times per week. This doesn't have to be more than a brisk walk or cycling around your neighborhood.

- Determine what form of exercise you like doing. Regardless of what you choose as your preferred option, it will be beneficial to a certain degree. It is better to stick to even low-impact exercise—which you enjoy and is sustainable for you—than opting for high-level activity, which you don't want and soon stop doing.

- Find a distraction when you exercise. Listen to a podcast or music and maybe even take along a friend; it will take your mind off how hard it is for you to exercise at the start.

- Commit yourself to your exercise plan by getting an exercise buddy. It is much harder to skip exercising for the day when you have someone who is keeping you accountable to show up and stick to your progress.

- Be kind to yourself. When you become impatient with your progress, remind yourself what motivated you in the first place to take up this routine. The primary purpose is to relieve the symptoms you are feeling and not to add stress to your plate.

Yoga as an Aid to Alleviate Anxiety

There are no alternatives to exercising when you want to grow strong and fit. Hard work and sweat are the only ways to achieve the desired outcome. When you wish to exercise your mind and increase its resilience to withstand the impact of stress and anxiety, yoga is one of the go-to options to achieve just that.

This statement is much more than a mere matter of personal opinion. There is sufficient evidence that proves that regular yoga sessions can actually enhance the brain' structure of participants. MRI scans reveal that those who regularly do yoga have a thicker layer around their cerebral cortex and hippocampus; both these areas of the brain are involved in higher-level thinking (Harvard Health Publishing [HHP], 2021b). The primary responsibility of the cerebral cortex is to process information, and the hippocampus is the center of memory and learning. Both these areas tend to shrink with age unless you do yoga. The same studies show the percentage of shrinkage in the brains of yogis is significantly less.

Beyond these antiaging properties, you'll also enjoy the same increased production of feel-good hormones as you'll gain from any other form of physical activity. However, yoga offers even more: Yoga increases the level of gamma-aminobutyric acid (GABA) in the brain, which is a chemical that elevates your mood and reduces anxiety (HHP, 2021b). While yoga on its own may not be enough to overcome anxiety, it is a complementary aid in treatment plans to overcome anxiety. It also serves as an excellent way to minimize your chances of experiencing anxiety in the first place.

Here, too, it will be of more significant benefit to commit yourself to shorter but regular yoga sessions than doing it for longer but less often. Initially, aim for only 10 minutes per day. As there are several types of yoga, you can explore and try various styles to see which works best for you. As always, if you enjoy what you are doing, sustaining this habit and enjoying the long-term benefits it brings is much easier.

Meditation as an Aid to Alleviate Anxiety

Meditation has been practiced for ages as a treasured aid to restore and maintain holistic health and wellness. It is, however, only due to more advanced technology, like functional magnetic resonance imaging (fMRI) and electroencephalogram (EEG), that researchers could determine that the practice is so powerful that it can change the brain's structure. It is one of the most effective ways to employ the mind-body connection in your favor. Therefore, meditation can fulfill an invaluable role in your journey to recovery as well as help you sustain a positive mindset. While meditation helps to improve the symptoms of anxiety, stress, and depression, you will also enjoy various added benefits: better concentration, improved attention, and a general improvement in your psychological wellness.

One of the most exciting studies exploring the benefits of meditation was done by researchers at Yale University. Their studies revealed that regular mindfulness meditation slows the activity in the brain's default mode network (DMN) (Walton, 2015). The DMN refers to the state we slip into while not being mindful of our thoughts. This state is also often referred to as the "monkey mind." It is the state we enter while we are not actively thinking about anything and simply allow our minds to wander. It is often the case that when this happens, our minds slip into a state of negativity and worrying. It is the perfect place for anxious thoughts to take control, and without even realizing what is happening, it can tumble us into a state of anxiety. As meditation slows down the activity in this area, it is less likely to cause us to enter such a state.

Another study completed by Johns Hopkins indicated that the effectiveness of meditation in reducing anxiety symptoms and treating the concern compared very well with the results delivered with the aid of antidepressants (Walton, 2015). Meditation is a much more viable and preferred long-term solution as no complications are linked to its practice. These results are possible through regular meditation and when it is employed as a form of brain training.

When used as a tool for improving our mental well-being, notable changes occur not to our mood, but to our brain as well. One of the ways how meditation changes the structure of the brain, reducing the symptoms of stress and anxiety, is that it reduces the amygdala size (Walton, 2015). The amygdala is the center of fear, stress, and anxiety. As meditation reduces the size of this area in the brain, it reduces the prevalence of these feelings.

In contrast to popular belief, meditation is not merely the practice of sitting and doing nothing. It requires a lot of effort to zoom your focus onto simply one subject and to maintain this focus. Initially, this can be challenging; many might even find it too hard. Therefore, only start with short sessions of about five minutes, and gradually increase the time you are meditating until you can achieve the outcome you desire.

There are several kinds of meditation you can try, but mindfulness meditation is often at the center of many research studies. Mindfulness meditation entails that you calm down your mind and let go of any negative thoughts by combining the practice of mindfulness with deep-breathing exercises. All you need to do is to find a quiet spot where you can sit undisturbed. Make sure you are comfortable and that there is nothing around that will distract you. Wear loose-fitting clothes and make sure you are comfortable. It will be handy to set a timer, so you can simply relax without needing to watch the clock. Take a few deep breaths and shift your focus onto your breathing. Become aware of how the air passes through your airways. Turn your thoughts to something positive. When your mind wanders to something else, just recognize these thoughts and push them away by replacing them with something positive. Be kind to yourself throughout. If you struggle, understand that it is normal, and you will eventually get there. Through consistency, you'll be able to move from five-minute sessions to holding this focus for much longer. Just know that the benefits it brings are highly beneficial and support your recovery and healing.

Takeaway

We've explored how the mind and body are connected. Through this connection, the mind can trigger a response in the body, causing it to experience higher levels of anxiety. This is a physical response caused by a mental process. We can utilize the same connection to calm the mind through physical actions. In this chapter, I shared several techniques you can employ to enjoy long-lasting reduced stress and anxiety levels.

Chapter Six

Forging New Habits

We are what we repeatedly do. Excellence, then, is not an act, but a habit. –Will Durant

For the longest time, we believed that change is only possible while the brain is still young and developing. We thought that after a certain age, there was no way you could ever learn any new behaviors. This belief presents itself in the saying that old dogs don't learn new tricks. Only now, when we know better, can we recognize this assumption as wrong and extremely limiting. To a great extent, it robbed many of the opportunity to improve and enhance their lives.

While nothing changed in the way we think or learn new habits, our understanding of what happens in the brain and the true nature of the brain's neuroplasticity opened an entirely new world. We know that hard neuroplastic change remains possible regardless of age. It is still the case that the juvenile brain is much more prone to these changes. We also know that change is not limited to only the young brain and that change can occur throughout the entire lifespan.

This enables us to create new habits and incorporate them into our lives at any age. Before we proceed and explore how we can instill these changes, we need to examine the nature of neuroplasticity in greater detail.

Understanding Neuroplasticity

Neuroplasticity, also known as brain plasticity, refers to the brain's ability to change by making new connections. In simpler terms, the brain can rewire itself and form new pathways. While it is far more common during the developmental stages in early life, these changes can occur at any time and are not limited to a specific age. This unique feature sets the brain apart from any other system that remains stagnant after establishing the initial network of connections.

These changes result from exposure to experiences, feelings, thoughts, and behavior. Neuroplasticity allows the brain to become more resilient and better equipped to deal with negative experiences, stress, and anxiety. It is also possible to rewire the brain to enjoy sustained mental wellness and combat the impact of anxiety. Neuroplasticity, in addition to reteaching it to respond differently, also benefits patients with brain injury, given that trauma to the brain can cause damage to the brain tissue. Through neuroplasticity, healing is possible to a certain extent.

Neuroplasticity is present in everyone and enables us to change and rewire our brains. Through this unique brain feature, we can all create new healthier habits and abandon the bad ones, including anxiety habits.

Exploring How Habits Hardwire Your Brain

Neuroplasticity depends on repeat behavior. For your brain to make these connections, you need to repeat certain behaviors until the brain has created the pathways. So, in a sense, neuroplasticity means that you can make changes. However, the changes you'll make still depend on the type of behavior you repeat. The speed and effectiveness with which you'll form these pathways to hardwire the brain will depend on how consistent you are in repeating the behavior you want to establish.

This would mean that if you are repeatedly stressing, pondering on the negative things in your life, overeating, drinking too much, putting off making changes and improvements in your life, watching pornography, or any other habitual behavior you have, you are hardwiring your brain to support these habits. If you are consciously trying to be more active, positive, focused, and determined, or any other healthy habit you want to instill, you are hardwiring your brain to support these actions. You can use neuroplasticity in any way you like, but whether you put it to use to benefit your life is entirely up to you. Therefore, it is incredibly vital that you are constantly aware of your mental state and responses, as these will become your neural traits.

What Is the Habit Loop?

The foundation of the habit loop is routine. This encompasses the things you repeatedly do without thinking about it at all; it includes tasks like brushing your teeth, taking out the garbage, having your morning coffee, or any other action you do without thinking. The habit loop also refers to behaviors like perpetual worrying, being negative, expecting the worst to happen or being positive, seeing opportunities rather than obstacles, or exercising regularly. It effectively reduces the workload on your conscious mind, requiring no active thinking. You have done the same things or behaved in the same manner enough times that your body and brain know precisely what is expected of them and how to proceed.

If these habits, which are on a loop in your life, are negative, they can keep you trapped in a negative cycle. By becoming aware of them and what you do, you can make conscious changes to what you will do. Initially, you may have to force yourself to stick to specific actions or repeat a behavior—this requires perseverance and consistency. Yet, once you've done it enough times, you've indicated adequately to your brain what is expected. With the support of neuroplasticity, you've hardwired your brain differently.

Another attribute of the brain you need to consider is that it doesn't distinguish between the types of information it stores. Sometimes, you can recall information you've been taught as a child, which played a vital role in forming you into the person you are today. Other times, it is the lyrics of a song you may have heard only a couple of times and still remember word for word. As the brain doesn't distinguish what type of information it stores, you need to be discerning how you encourage it to store information.

The basal ganglion is a part of the brain located in its frontal part. It is the location of automatic learning and where habit cycles are created. While habit cycles or loops can benefit your life in many ways, it also holds the potential to fuel your anxiety and keep you in a depressed state.

Habit loops consist of three components. To effectively use these components, you need to understand what they are and how they work to obtain the desired results.

The Cue

The cue is the trigger that sets the entire process of a habit in motion. An example of a cue is when you wake up, which triggers your habit of walking to the kitchen and pouring your first cup of coffee. Watching a movie serves as a cue to have snacks around. Coming back home from work can be a cue that you need to take your dog for a walk.

Cues come in different forms and can be linked to time, an emotional state, people, location, or the last thing you did.

The Routine

The routine refers to the actual process of taking action. It refers to what the cue tells you to do: making coffee, snacking, or taking your dog for a walk. When hardwiring your brain to support positive habits, the routine refers to the action or response you would like to have in your life which will benefit you.

The Reward

The reward is what keeps you coming back for more. It can be the first sip of your coffee, as it is strong in aroma and answers your body's craving for caffeine; the sweet or salty taste of the snacks you love to enjoy; or the fresh air and seeing your dog's excitement to get out of the house. These are all rewards, and they play a crucial role in changing any human behavior. Yet, it is not only humans who are prone to live their lives according to these habit loops.

Pavlov's Dogs

I don't think explaining how habit loops work without mentioning Pavlov's dogs is possible. The Russian experimental neurologist, physiologist, and psychologist Ivan Pavlov lived from the late 1800s to the early 1900s. He did groundbreaking work in the field of classical conditioning. Pavlov's studies initially focused on how dogs start to salivate when they see food. Soon, he realized that these dogs didn't even have to see the food to secrete more saliva as they already did when they merely heard the footsteps of his assistant bringing them their food.

He also introduced a bell system where he would ring a bell before feeding the dogs. Later, the dogs would start to respond as if they were being fed merely by hearing the bells ring. In this experiment, the bell would be the trigger, the saliva secretion the routine, and getting food the reward (Mcleod, 2021). His experiments demonstrate that the more you repeat the same loop, the stronger the wiring in your mind becomes, thanks to neuroplasticity.

Anxiety loops are formed in the exact same manner. If you repetitively overreact to stressors, these stressors become your triggers for increased anxiety. Being anxious or highly stressed turns into a routine, and taking the action necessary to avoid this stressor, gives you a reward. While this may limit your life, there is still the sensation that you were able to avoid the emotional stress, and the relief you experience makes it all worthwhile.

For example, knowing that you must attend your neighbor's wedding can be a stressor. You feel insecure and don't want to be around so many strangers. Having to dress up and attend the event increases your anxiety. You devise a feeble excuse for not going, even though you know our neighbor would love to have you there—this is your routine. Once you've declined the invitation, you feel a sense of relief. You've taken the necessary action to avoid this emotional distress, which serves as your reward. The next time you are invited to an event, you follow the same routine and strengthen the pathways establishing social anxiety in your mind.

Changing Your Brain's Wiring Through Behavioral Changes

The only way to change the wiring system in your brain is by changing your behavior. It is how you can create new pathways, and as the old pathways become less used, they gradually fade away.

This would demand that you rely on the prefrontal cortex to make a conscious decision to follow a different routine. It requires that you set your intention to break this habit and think about how you would like to behave as a response to a particular trigger. Initially, this won't feel comfortable as you are treading new and different paths. You can almost compare the process to breaking new ground. Let's say your brain is a garden with several well-trodden pathways. It is easy to follow these paths as you are familiar with their layout. You need to create new paths when you want to change your habits. You would have to determine where you would want these paths to lead and what would be the best route to take you there. Maybe you need to dig up the lawn or go through established beddings to get there. At first, this can be a slow process, but the more you walk down these new paths, the more established they become. As you are no longer treading on the old paths, the grass eventually takes over and covers them, so you can hardly see where the old paths once were. When you've walked down these paths often enough, they are established and set, just like the wiring in your brain.

How often you would walk down these paths would determine how long the process would take to establish all these new paths. The entire process can take only three weeks for some, but for others, it may take a little longer. When we stop for a moment to think that so many anxiety symptoms can be avoided simply through this simplistic process, overcoming this major obstacle in your life becomes a lot easier.

Creating New Habit Loops in a Few Easy Steps

There is nothing really hard or complex about changing your habit loops, as it only requires consistency and perseverance.

Identify Who You Want to Be

Before making any changes, you must determine who you want to become. Your habits and identity are intrinsically linked to each other, and you can't change one without changing the other. Thus, if you want your identity to define you as a non-anxious person, you must act that way. This will guide you to identify and forge the habits which will manifest your chosen identity.

Identify Your Triggers

What are the cues that trigger a specific response in your mind? By using mindfulness and keeping a journal to track your behavior, you can identify the triggers that set you off into a downward spiral. You can also use the same techniques to determine what cues cause an increase in dopamine to motivate you to take the necessary action. The best approach would be to remove any triggers in your life, but this may sometimes mean that you need to relocate or find a new job, which isn't always financially viable or physically possible. However, you must ensure that your environment supports your efforts to create new habits. Thus, make as many small changes as possible if you can't make any new ones.

Identify Your Routines

The second component of the habit loop is your response to your triggers. Once you've identified your triggers, you need to determine what response you would need to have on these triggers that will complement and enforce your newly chosen identity. If you are establishing your identity as a non-anxious person, then your routines need to be in line with this identity, suited to the habits of someone who is non-anxious.

How Will You Reward Yourself?

What would you consider a reward to encourage you to repeat the same habit loop needed to establish your life's new, positive habit? Identify what would be a reward to you, encouraging you to keep up with the behavior which may initially feel uncomfortable.

Repeat, Repeat, Repeat

There is only one way to establish new habits with the help of neuroplasticity, and that is to repeat a certain action or process repeatedly so that it doesn't feel strange or uncomfortable anymore. You need to be so at ease with the new habits that you don't even have to think about them anymore.

Minimize Your Stress Levels

It is often the case that bad habits form as ways to relieve stress. Let's revert to you missing out on your neighbor's wedding as a way to escape the stress of your experience when confronted with social gatherings. When you identify alternative ways to deal with your stress, you no longer need to employ these toxic habits.

There are many ways you can choose from your preferred form of stress relief. These techniques run the gamut from physical fitness to quieter activities: jogging a few miles to simply blowing off steam to meditation, yoga, writing in your gratitude journal, or even taking a nap. Identify the steps you need to take to reduce your stress levels and see how you can incorporate these steps more often in your life. Once relying on old and toxic habits is no longer necessary, you will feel less inclined to revert to them.

Be More Mindful

One of the sad realities of life is that it can pass us by without us ever really taking note of it. We can become so consumed in what we believe is essential that we just slip into autopilot and forget to think about life and how it makes us feel. This is when our brain operates on autopilot and robs us of the opportunity to think about what is good for us and what habits we need to change to live our desired lives.

Become more mindful and aware of what is happening in your life and what you would like your life to be like. Engage your prefrontal cortex and start to make more active decisions, rather than just slipping into old patterns and allowing your subconscious thinking to take over. If you don't think about what you are doing, it can be easy to find yourself where you've precisely done what you don't want to do, as your brain simply reacts as per usual on a particular cue.

Take Small but Consistent Steps

Change demands willpower. Willpower gets depleted as it is like a muscle that gets tired after working for some time. The demand on your willpower to remain consistent can be too much if you start by making many significant changes. Thus, start by making small and constant changes that aren't as demanding and more sustainable.

You can also replenish your willpower with serotonin. You'll feel more confident and significant when your serotonin levels are high. Both contribute to strengthening your willpower to continue carving out new pathways even when it is hard to do.

Boost Your Serotonin Levels

Besides increasing your willpower, serotonin also supports the prefrontal cortex to function optimally. Therefore, you must ensure you do what is necessary to replenish your serotonin reserves.

There are a variety of ways to boost your serotonin. Spending time in the sunlight, thinking happy thoughts, and doing things you enjoy can all contribute to increasing your serotonin. Other helpful aids also range from getting enough exercise, to even receiving massages. All of these steps will contribute to increasing your serotonin levels as additional aids along with a healthy gut, which remains a key contributor to sustaining an optimal serotonin level.

Make Your Life a Priority You Think About

The more you think about your life and employ your prefrontal cortex to create patterns to support the life you desire, the more you will move in the direction you choose. Become more mindful, include regular affirmations in your routine, and engage in positive self-talk. A vision board can be another helpful aid to imagining and manifesting the life you desire. One of the most effective ways to achieve the life you desire remains to actively think about it and work on getting it. Once we simply slip into autopilot, our lives and dreams begin to take a nosedive into the dark depths of anxiety and depression.

Celebrate More Often

Don't celebrate your goals, but do celebrate your accomplishments. You can share goals with someone you trust to help you stay accountable for what you've set out to do. However, regardless of how small your victory on this journey is, celebrate it. By celebrating our small victories, we gain confidence that we'll be able to achieve much more significant accomplishments too. Every milestone you reach takes you a step or two closer to your big goal. Being mindful of our successes is a good way to reward the brain for good behavior, so make every achievement count.

Take Stock of Your Crowd

When I refer to "your crowd," I mean the people you spend most of your time with. This will include your family, friends, coworkers, and acquaintances. Who are the people you mingle with at work? Consider the conversations you are part of during breaks, next to the field when you watch your children partake in sports, and at the shops when you bump into people you know. Are these people the right people to help you achieve your goal of overcoming anxiety? You need to become aware of the nature of the conversations you engage in. It will be impossible to remain positive if you often surround yourself with people who only focus on the negative things in life. Therefore, ensure their nature and the nature of your conversations are beneficial to your efforts to break free from stress, anxiety, and depression.

Consider the people you spend time with as part of your environment and surround yourself with people who encourage you, offer support and keep you accountable for your goals. These are the people who are your support network and the ones you should include in your crowd. If this is not the case for you, it is time to create some distance between yourself and the naysayers in your life.

Takeaway

Neuroplasticity is the pathway to achieving the desired outcome when we want to forge new habits. It refers to the brain's ability to form new connections. These connections are what would determine our behavior, response, and reactions once triggered by emotional cues. While your brain may be hardwired to respond in a specific manner that only increases your anxiety, you maintain the ability to change this to your favor. Once you've identified how you would like to change your identity, you need to determine the triggers, responses, and rewards that are synonymous with the identity you seek. The only thing left to do is to repeat these cycles as often as necessary to establish new pathways and change how your brain is wired.

Chapter Seven

Professional Solutions and Limits

*Science cannot solve the ultimate mystery of nature.
And that is because, in the last analysis, we ourselves
are a part of the mystery that we are trying to solve.*
–Max Planck

Anxiety is a global concern affecting the lives of millions of people. Therefore, it is only natural to expect that there are more than just a few professional solutions available to address this widespread issue. As we progress on our exploration of all these means, it will become evident that each of these solutions has limitations. While you can benefit from these solutions, there will always be certain areas that are lacking. Here, you can employ the alternative options explained in this book to fill the gaps. I would never recommend that you step away from professional treatment and only opt for alternative solutions. The solutions I've expanded on can also remedy stress's effect on your life and prevent anxiety or depression from getting a foothold in your mindset.

The most widely used remedies for anxiety are psychotherapy and medication. In some instances, professionals would rely on both means to address the concerns. However, you must depend on your health professional's advice to find the best solution. It would require a relationship of authenticity and trust between you and your healthcare provider to aid the expert in the field to guide you along with the most effective solution to help you get your life back. Given the unique nature of each case, it is up to you to decide when is the best time to reach out for professional care.

Nevertheless, if you've already tried to obtain the desired results from alternative solutions and are still struggling to gain control over your life, I would recommend that you seek professional help sooner rather than later. If you are feeling overwhelmed and cannot cope with the pressure of life, don't delay getting the support you need.

Exploring Psychotherapy

Psychotherapy is conventionally understood as a type of talk therapy where someone can have regular therapy sessions to discuss their mindset and the challenges it brings to their daily life. This kind of therapy is aimed at a specific mental health concern. It works most effectively if the therapy addresses specific anxiety and the needs it creates in one's life. Psychotherapy can be divided into different subcategories.

Cognitive Behavioral Therapy

Cognitive behavioral therapy (CBT) focuses on thought patterns and how to identify and address negative thinking patterns as a means to change destructive behavior. It also covers emotional responses. CBT aims to empower you to change your negative thoughts and reactions from negative to positive to enable you to overcome your challenges.

Often, without even realizing it, you can harbor profound negativity in your mind. This will taint all your thoughts and experiences with negativity, increasing and worsening your anxiety and depression symptoms. The support and guidance of a CBT professional will enable you to identify and challenge these negative thoughts. It is how you can determine their validity and replace them with positive and constructive thoughts and responses. CBT has a long-standing reputation as a highly effective way to address depression and anxiety and has been proven to help depression and anxiety patients to be less anxious, stressed, or worried (Holland, 2022).

Exposure Therapy

This type of CBT is mainly used as a treatment option for those suffering from anxiety disorders stemming from a specific fear, like social anxiety. Here, the goal is to help patients to confront the fears in which their anxiety disorder is rooted. In practice, this means that patients will acquire the tools to face situations they usually avoid. Exposure therapy includes relaxation exercises as this would serve as a coping tool to face anxiety-causing problems effectively (Holland, 2022).

Acceptance and Commitment Therapy

Acceptance and commitment therapy (ACT) will be a recommended treatment option if you suffer from specific anxiety disorders like obsessive-compulsive disorder (OCD) or social anxiety. The focus of this treatment is to help you to recognize and acknowledge your values. The second step would be to provide you with the needed tools to adjust your behavior in a manner suitable to express your values. The treatment option depends heavily on creating mindfulness and is primarily used in collaboration with other treatment techniques. No matter the technique, incorporating a goal helps you achieve the desired outcome.

Dialectical Behavioral Therapy

Do you sometimes feel that your thoughts and the situations in which you have them are standing in opposition to each other? Dialectical behavioral therapy (DBT) can be a helpful treatment if this is the case. Here, professionals rely heavily on exercises to establish an increased awareness to improve your distress tolerance and emotional regulation. The therapy also attends to your interpersonal skills and enhances them to an optimal level. DBT is often a recommended treatment option to address panic disorder, GAD, OCD, and post-traumatic stress disorder (PTSD) (Holland, 2022).

Eye Movement Desensitization and Reprocessing

Enduring a traumatic experience or suffering through long-term trauma would require support to help the brain heal. During eye movement desensitization and reprocessing (EMDR), your therapist would use specific eye movement exercises, tones, or a range of methods to achieve bilateral stimulation, allowing your brain to reprocess hurtful memories.

The treatment can benefit a range of concerns, from dealing effectively with phobias, panic disorders, and PTSD, to name only a few mindset concerns (Holland, 2022).

Interpersonal Therapy

The core focus of interpersonal therapy (IPT) is how you function within social settings, specifically within your relationships with others. During IPT, you would work with the professional to address the issues you are facing that are keeping you from sustaining lasting and happy relationships. IPT will also help you to adjust easier to changes in your social role, manage any grief, and address conflict productively.

Originally, IPT served as a treatment option merely to address depression. As it progressed, it became evident that it is also helpful in managing anxiety, especially social anxiety (Holland, 2022).

Medication

The first and most important thing you need to know about medication is that it doesn't heal anxiety. While medication can ease the symptoms, it never addresses the cause of your concerns. Eradicating the roots of anxiety and depression in your life requires work on your end to become familiar with the coping mechanisms to help you through anxiety. In the end, the tools, skills, changes in your habits, alterations to your diet, and living a balanced lifestyle will truly make the difference you seek. That said, none of these solutions will deliver instant results, and medication can only ease the symptoms you're experiencing until you can better take on your challenges.

Medication for anxiety can be divided into antidepressants and psychiatric medication. You can only use these medications when working with a professional to treat your anxiety, as all antidepressants would require a professional to prescribe them to you. Also, only certain professionals who have specialized training are legally allowed to prescribe psychiatric medication.

Dr. Rahul Khurana (n.d.) explains the different types of medication you may come across as part of your recovery program.

Selective Serotonin Reuptake Inhibitors

Familiar names in this category are Prozac, Zoloft, Paxil, Lexapro, Luvox, and Celexa. These names are the popular go-to solutions for treating the symptoms of depression and anxiety. The conventional term we use to refer to these kinds of drugs is "antidepressants." Still, this is a relatively poor classification, as they are far more specialized than merely addressing the symptoms of depression.

For example, Zoloft is a familiar brand for the active ingredient sertraline. This is an FDA-approved drug to treat PTSD, major depression, OCD, premenstrual dysphoric disorder, and panic disorder. We also need to consider that while sertraline is approved by the FDA for these conditions, it can also be used for many other conditions, referred to as "off-label purposes." Usually, this is because getting FDA approval is very expensive. Even when these drugs aren't FDA-approved for all conditions, professionals are aware of what these drugs are capable of and can subscribe to a drug to address a specific concern without having FDA approval. Doing this is legal in the US, but the mental health care professional must explain this to the patient.

All the drugs that fall into this category have the potential to bring about immediate improvement, yet, in some instances, it can take from three to eight weeks before you will experience the level of improvement you desire. The difference in time depends mainly on the state of the person taking them. Overall, these drugs are primarily generic and quite affordable. Another benefit to medicines in this category is that they have been around for quite some time, making them a safer option given that all possible side effects are known and recorded. These drugs also have fewer and less severe side effects, and the severity of the impact of these side effects will vary according to the sensitivity of the person taking them. I urge you never to discontinue any drugs without your doctor's guidance on weaning off, as you can develop discontinuation syndrome. This concern is more severe in certain antidepressants than in others.

Serotonin-Norepinephrine Reuptake Inhibitors

Effexor, Pristiq, Fetzima, Cymbalta, and Savella are the most widely available brands here. These drugs are very similar to the previous type discussed. The most profound difference is that they increase the level of noradrenaline and serotonin in the brain. Some of these drugs also have the FDA's approval to be utilized as pain medication.

Benzodiazepines

Xanax, Ativan, and Valium all fall under this category. They are fast-acting solutions delivering results in minutes. The most prominent concern with this type of drug is that it has a long half-life, meaning it can create a cumulative effect over the first couple of weeks. They are also highly addictive and can be fatal when you take them with alcohol. More recent studies also revealed a link between the long-term use of benzodiazepines and dementia, but this evidence is still inconclusive (Khurana, 2019).

Buspirone

Buspirone is a drug like no other and works wonders to alleviate the symptoms of generalized anxiety. It can even be used to treat depression when taken with antidepressants. The drug effectively changes how noradrenaline, serotonin, dopamine, and the GABA systems impact the brain. You will have to use the drug for about a month or two before noticing any improvement.

Beta-Blockers

Beta-blockers are prescribed to treat anxiety as an off-label treatment option. It means that the FDA doesn't recognize beta-blockers as a treatment for anxiety, although it does bring relief to the symptoms you may experience. The most common application of this drug is to address the symptoms of social anxiety and performance anxiety. Beta-blockers are nonaddictive, and they don't have any cognitive side effects linked to them. Beta-blockers are often prescribed to patients with high blood pressure to alleviate this condition. It would mean that if you have low blood pressure, it is best to stay clear of beta-blockers. There has also been an association between beta-blockers and worsened depression symptoms; more research is required to settle the matter (Khurana, 2019).

Other Medication

These aren't the only available antidepressants on the market. While I don't deem it necessary to go into these options with as much detail, it remains essential to mention that most options have a sedative effect. Thus, the best time to take them would be before bedtime to help you sleep better. Although some users mention that they feel like they have a hangover the following day after taking these antidepressants, the effectiveness and the severity of the possible side effects vary from person to person.

Tricyclic Antidepressants

Now, we are looking at a much older type of antidepressant. The most prominent concern with this drug is that it can increase cardiac risk. Therefore, elderly patients should stay away from this specific option. The drug would increase the level of serotonin in the body and that of norepinephrine. They can also serve as pain blockers, so they may be a good option if your anxiety occurs with pain.

Monoamine Oxidase Inhibitors

This type also falls into the category of older types of antidepressants. Their general purpose is to increase brain serotonin, norepinephrine, and dopamine levels. They are effective, and some people respond better to these antidepressants than the more modern versions. What counts against these drugs is that they severely restrict your diet. When you use monoamine oxidase inhibitors (MAOIs), you have to avoid eating certain types of meat, cheese, dairy products, alcohol, fish, and food that contains yeast—these food restrictions are the main reason they are used less often. However, you can use them in the form of a patch, and this will allow tiny doses of the drug.

Bupropion (Wellbutrin or Zyban)

Zyban may be a familiar name to smokers keen on quitting the habit. It works on your levels of dopamine and noradrenaline but does not affect serotonin levels. This type of drug is also commonly used for the treatment of attention deficit disorder (ADD) and attention deficit hyperactivity disorder (ADHD). However, if you have a medical history of bulimia or seizures, it is best to avoid the drug.

S-Adenosylmethionine

S-adenosylmethionine (SAMe) is naturally present in our bodies. As a drug, it serves several purposes; it helps hormone regulation and treats depression. Until now, there hasn't been conclusive evidence that it is a beneficial aid to treat anxiety.

Antihistamines

The impact of antihistamines can be very limited, but they hold the potential to bring some relief. The most common side effect of antihistamines is that they make you drowsy and can be addictive.

Antipsychotics

This type of drug is not approved by the FDA to be used for anxiety disorders. They are primarily used to treat mental concerns like schizophrenia or bipolar disorders.

Others Substances

Psychedelics

Under this category, you'll find hallucinogens like magic mushrooms. While they may hold the potential to alleviate the symptoms of depression, there is still a lot of prejudice against them, preventing comprehensive research. Thus, it needs further research before we can make conclusive statements about its effectiveness.

Cannabidiol and Medical Marijuana

Perspectives on the benefits and risks of marijuana are still highly controversial. Over recent years, there has been increasing research to determine the actual benefits of marijuana and the role it can play in alleviating anxiety symptoms; also, it can be addictive to some. Yet, it predominantly has far fewer side effects than many other prescriptions, and there has never been a fatality due to a marijuana overdose.

Typically, marijuana can be divided into two types of products: cannabidiol (CBD) and tetrahydrocannabinol (THC). CBD is not psychotic and will not have the same impact as products containing THC. THC is psychotic, limiting the time you can use the product to alleviate your anxiety symptoms.

The use of marijuana to treat anxiety still requires further research in much greater detail. More studies would also reveal which strains are more effective in treating symptoms. Nonetheless, for now, I would say there is enough proof to consider this type of drug a viable solution to treat anxiety.

The Limits of Medical Treatment Options Addressing Anxiety Symptoms

As I've stated earlier, medication can improve but not address the source of the symptoms you are experiencing, especially if your anxiety, stress, and depression are rooted in poor lifestyle choices; sustaining bad habits; hosting harmful and destructive thoughts; and poor nutrition. While medication is a helpful aid to support you on your healing journey, it is not the sole solution you can turn to and expect a complete recovery from. Below are some of the main reasons behind the limitations of the use of medication for treating anxiety:

- Everyone has a unique biological composition. This means that the same chemical solution presented in a drug will affect everyone differently. While specific outcomes are present in enough cases that we can consider it an expected effect of the drug, your biological composition may be more or less sensitive to the active ingredients. This will impact the effectiveness of its usage.

- Your body often develops a higher tolerance towards the active ingredients after long-term use. When this happens, your body doesn't respond as well any longer to the drug, and you would need to take higher concentrations or larger doses. The solutions sound easy enough, but higher doses also increase the chances of suffering from the side effects or developing an addiction to the drug.

- Side effects from the drugs can be too severe and do more harm than good. The chances of this happening will again depend on the biological composition of the person taking the drugs.

- The powerful effect of some drugs on your emotions may block out every other emotional sensation. It can be tough to address the causes of your emotional concerns when all feelings are numbed out. For some, this numbed state can even turn into a comfort zone where they feel no need to do the work and face the causes of their anxiety or depression.

While we should never underestimate the role of medication in anxiety treatment, it is also vital to remember that this is not the one and only solution available. There is also the odd chance that it may not be your most effective treatment option.

Takeaway

Anxiety is an immense and growing global concern. Understandably, addressing this concern is of utmost importance to the pharmaceutical industry as there is such a high demand for instant solutions. This chapter has explored the many different types of medication your health professional can prescribe. Still, there is one concern limiting them all:

Medication only relieves the symptoms you experience and won't resolve the cause of your anxiety. Freeing yourself of the impact of stress, anxiety, and depression requires a holistic approach demanding that you attend to every aspect of your being.

Chapter Eight

Support Network

We only have what we give. –Isabelle Allende

Anxiety can leave you feeling extremely isolated. This can be the case even if you have friends and family to turn to for support. It may feel that even if they want to help you, they simply don't grasp what you are going through or what you need from them. If this is the situation you find yourself in, or if you simply don't have anyone to turn to, it will benefit you to join a formal support group. Here, you can share your experiences with others who are having similar experiences and receive the guidance, support and help you need.

Support groups can take on the form of in-person sessions or online. Many support groups have professionals taking the lead, but it is not a requirement for any support group. So, when you are getting advice within a group that is not given by a professional, it is best to apply caution when using it. Never consider your attendance to a support group as a replacement for treatment.

It is often the case that people only seek support when going through tough times. Despite that, we all need help, even when things are going well. It is why the most successful people in life also have a support group or network they can lean on during challenging times. Therefore, regardless of whether your symptoms are severe or still manageable, you will benefit from having access to trusted support.

How to Find a Support Group

Who are the people you can rely on during challenging times? By identifying the people who are always there for you, you already have the first set of people organically part of your support group. They may be family, friends, or coworkers, and it can also be that you are already regularly calling on a counselor or therapist; these professionals will be part of your network. Also, if you have spiritual leaders, mentors, coaches, or even teachers who fit the profile, they can also contribute to your support group.

When forming your support group, consider including as many people as possible. This will help to share the responsibility among many, rather than overburdening only a few. Also, aim for a diverse group—it is always better to have people you can rely on of all ages, cultures, backgrounds, and professions. This will ensure diversity in the feedback and support you get.

Seeking the support of a professional healthcare provider is often something many would shy away from. This is primarily due to skewed perspectives, as there is no difference between calling on a mental healthcare professional and your general practitioner. Especially if you are struggling to overcome anxiety, the support of such a professional can be invaluable to you.

Benefits of a Support Network

- You can enjoy several benefits when you have a support network to rely on.

- Within this group, you get encouragement to take and continue the steps needed for recovery and to reclaim control over your life.

- A support group offers security, as simply knowing you are not alone and that you have a group you can call on can be enough to get you through a range of anxiety symptoms.

- The group will also keep you accountable to continue with the steps you need to take to overcome your challenges.

- A trusted support group is there to help you carry your

burdens when they become too much for you to do on your own.

- The group provides you with a sense of belonging and that you are part of something larger than yourself or the anxiety you are facing.

- A support group is considered highly beneficial to sustain a healthy mental state. It appears to be especially helpful to women, patients, students, and more mature adults.

Exploring the Structure of a Support Group

The most important person in any support group is always you. It would mean that you must be mentally committed to sharing your burdens and making yourself vulnerable to others. The support group won't benefit you if you do not share or aren't present during these conversations.

Any of the following can serve as effective support groups, or you can enjoy a combination of these options:

- a few close friends
- your family
- informal groups meeting in your community
- formal therapy groups led by a professional

- online support groups and chats

You Should Support Yourself Too

It is often the case that you are your own most influential supporter, yet we sometimes fail to see this. Therefore, I want to remind you of why it is so vital that you actively become your own greatest supporter.

There will be times when you are alone and have to deal with your anxiety all by yourself. So, while your support group will be beneficial to you, you can't depend on others alone to overcome this obstacle in your way. You need to establish the coping mechanisms to get you through these tough times when there is nobody to reach out to.

Other people know you based on your behavior, words, and responses. Nevertheless, you are the only one familiar with your thoughts and feelings. You understand yourself better than anyone else. So, you are the only one who truly understands your anxiety and your goals for overcoming it. The answers to all the questions you need to live a happy and content life is inside of you. You are the only one with the answers you need to overcome your anxiety.

The more you progress in overcoming your anxiety, the more confident you'll become in your belief that you can beat it. You have the strengths needed to overcome the obstacle, and you can if you believe in your ability to do so.

Help is essential in your progress toward beating anxiety, but always rely on support groups, professional treatment, medication, and every tip provided in this book as tools to help you overcome your challenge. Regardless of this, though, remember that you are at the center of everything, ensuring you get the desired results.

When Should You Build Your Support Network?

It is far too familiar that people only start building a support network when they need help, feel trapped, or are even disempowered. While building your network is never too late, the optimal time to do so is during shared, positive experiences. This is when you can invest in a group and find individuals you trust, giving you the certainty they'll be there when you need them. The key to a sustained healthy mindset is to follow a similar approach as when you want to enjoy sustained physical health. You need to take preventative care to ensure longevity. Creating a strong support network, even when you are emotionally fit and in a great mental space, would serve the same purpose as going for a regular physical checkup and sustaining a healthy lifestyle. Regular visits with a mental health professional would be beneficial to ensure that you remain on track with your mental health goals.

How to Strengthen Your Support Network

Except for yourself, your entire support group consists of people. They are human too; suffer challenges and setbacks in life; have days when they need support; and would need to rely on you. Therefore, you mustn't only withdraw from this group but make regular deposits too. This is in the form of appreciation and emotional support when needed is how you can fortify your support network. The following tips will serve to guide you along the way:

- Always keep in touch with the members of your support group.

- Express your appreciation and how much they mean to you.

- They may need you too; make sure you are available when they do.

- Celebrate the successes of your group members.

- Show your respect for their needs, limits, and boundaries.

- Make sure communication can flow at all times.

- Cut the ties when a relationship within this group doesn't work for you.

- Remember that they want to support you, so accept the

help they offer.

Takeaway

A support group can help you through challenging times and provide the support you need to sustain your mental health. Therefore, if you don't already have a support group, start building one now. Reach out to the people there for you and strengthen those bonds. Always remember that you are the most important person in your support group, so make sure you are present when reaching out to your support team.

As you may not always be able to reach out to your support group, you would need to learn coping skills to help you through tough times on your own. We'll explore some of the most trusted coping skills you can employ in our next chapter.

Chapter Nine

Coping Techniques

If the problem can be solved why worry? If the problem cannot be solved worrying will do you no good.
–Shantideva

In the previous chapter, I mentioned that while support networks play a crucial role in your recovery and sustaining a healthy mindset, you can't become entirely dependent on your network. You need specific coping mechanisms to help you get through the moment when anxiety spikes. These techniques will empower you to take control when you feel vulnerable. They serve as a way to regain your confidence, the kind of confidence I want to send you off with. Therefore, I felt this is fitting for the final chapter of the book.

Using Breathing

When you go into a state of anxiety, your breathing changes. While breathing takes place autonomously, we can take control of our breathing to change our state of mind. Through this breathing technique, you can take control and calm your mind and improve anxiety symptoms.

Simply start by taking a few deep breaths. Breathe deeply, hold your breath for a few counts, and slowly exhale.

Once you've done this a couple of times, you can switch to the 5-5-5 breathing method: Simply breathe in slowly for five counts. Then, hold your breath for five counts and follow by exhaling for five counts. This is a much slower form of breathing, and it demands you shift your focus away from your symptoms. The technique has an instant calming effect. It is an effective way to stop your stress response, and you can use it anywhere.

While the technique is helpful during moments of high stress, it serves as a method to reduce your stress levels in general. Use the technique as many times as you like whenever you have a free moment during your day. You will enjoy optimal results when you repeat the exercise 10–15 times daily.

Combining Breathing and Smiling

Breathing and smiling can have a powerful impact if employed together. This is one of the many golden nuggets James Clear shares in his book Atomic Habits. He explains a technique to use smiling and breathing to experience an instant increase in joy.

First, you need to think about something that genuinely makes you happy. This can be anything from biting into your favorite treat to cuddling with your cat. Once you have identified what it is, breathe deeply, smile, and do it. So, if biting into a specific chocolate bar makes you happy, get the bar, breathe, smile, and bite into it. Repeat the exercise several times. Eventually, your brain will have formed the pathways linking smiling and breathing with a sense of happiness. Once this habit is hardwired, you can simply breathe, smile, and feel instant pleasure without even having your treat. Use this technique whenever your stress level increases or you feel down.

Use Your Senses to Calm Yourself Down

Using your five senses to combat the symptoms of anxiety and stress is another helpful and widely-trusted technique to enjoy greater tranquility and happiness. The method demands greater awareness of your present environment. It then shifts your focus away from the negativity you may be lingering on to being more positive.

Sit down and breathe a couple of times deeply. Then scan your environment:

- Name five things you can see
- List four things you can feel
- Identify three things you can hear

- Name two things you can smell

- List one thing you can taste

Using Mindfulness

A lot of the stress and anxiety we experience stems from our inability to be mentally present in the present moment. Our minds wander into the past and linger on regrets, or bounce off into the future where there is much to stress about. By being more mindful, we can bring our minds back to the present moment. This present moment doesn't contain any stress and is a calm place.

Close your eyes before taking a few deep breaths. Focus on the way your body is feeling at the moment. Become aware of your heartbeat pushing the blood through your veins. Be mindful of the breeze on your skin, whether it is warm or if it causes a sensation of your clothes touching your body. What is your belly feeling like? Take note of the air passing through your airways.

Now, move your focus away from yourself to your environment. What can you hear, smell, and feel? Take note of every bit of information passing through your senses and into your awareness. Once you've observed your environment with your eyes closed, shift back to yourself and the sensations in your body.

Repeat the exercise of shifting from yourself to the environment and back. Repeating this exercise will make you more confident in managing your focus and blocking out your physical sensations. It is how you will become better at blocking fears and concerns about unfounded catastrophes and feel more empowered to manage your environment.

Get to Know Your Anger

It is possible to acknowledge the anger you are feeling without showing it.

This exercise will aid you in mastering this skill. When you feel upset, grab a pen and paper and write down the following question, "If I was angry, what would I be angry about?"

Now, give your mind the freedom to come up with any possible thing you may be angry about. Except for keeping your sentences short, you have the freedom to write about anything. You'll notice that as soon as you get going, a matter may surface that you didn't even consider. This exercise is a beautiful way to get rid of anger and to understand the relationship between your anger and anxiety.

Indulge in Fun

When was the last time you played? As we grow up and mature, playing and having fun disappear from our lives. We become serious adults, suffering from adult concerns like stress and anxiety. Having a good laugh can serve as a great form of stress relief. Thus, remind yourself of the things you enjoyed doing, and then indulge in having a little fun and a good laugh.

Turn Off Your Mind

Don't you sometimes wish that you could just turn off your mind like you would with your car's engine? It sounds like the most convenient solution when the brain is overheating because of all the stress you put it through. The good news is that you can do just that—you can make an active decision to calm your mind or simply relax.

Find a place where you can sit relaxed. Close your eyes and visualize an open container. Prepare yourself to receive what is coming to mind. Then, allow your problems to filter into your mind and place them into this container as they do. Once you've done this in your visualization, these problems are all "gone," and you never have to think about them again. Once you are done, place the lid on the container, so that these problems can remain contained. Only return to the box if you are actively going to resolve one of these concerns for good.

Consistently Bring Back Your Wandering Mind

Sometimes, our minds have a will of their own and continue to wander even when we've brought it back to the present moment. You need to be consistent in doing so every time you find it wandering and pondering on the negative. This is the only way you can change your mind's loop and establish a new pattern for it to follow. Even though it is impossible to simply keep our minds from thinking, we can still consistently redirect them back to the present moment and create new ways for them to behave.

Stop Worrying Indefinitely

Our worries can be real, and we need to face them head-on. When you come across specific concerns, it is best to worry about them and address and resolve them straight away. Then, there is no need for secondary worrying to consume your mind later. By taking this approach, you have much greater control over the entire worrying process and can much better control it. The following method will help you achieve this.

1. List all the things you need to worry about. Then, give yourself a time limit for worrying. Let's say that for 10–20 minutes, you'll be committed to worrying, but when the time expires, you are done with it.

2. Follow by doing the things you can address right away. By checking them off your list, you'll have fewer things on your list the next time you decide to worry.

3. Identify when your next worrying session will be and create an entry in your diary for that time.

4. Whenever anything comes to mind urging you to

worry about it, you know it is one of two cases: Either you've already worried about it, or you need to schedule this for your next worry session.

It will also help to have a list of things that can divert your mind from worrying about something positive. Pick something from this list and shift your focus toward it.

Address the Causes of Your Anxiety

Creating a plan would require you to set a goal in mind and devise a way to achieve this goal. While this might require that you make some changes to your initial plan, once you have your completed plan, you don't have to make constant changes. This is the most noticeable difference between having a plan and a worrying brain. A brain immersed in worry constantly doubts itself and changes its plan. There is immense uncertainty about whether this is the best course of action. As the mind examines itself, it needs constant reassurance.

1. When you become a planning expert, you can overcome the challenges of a worrying mind present. By following these simple steps, you can end your worries as you will have a good plan.

2. Identify and define the issues you are dealing with.

3. Compile a list of all the solutions you can follow.

4. Pick one of these solutions.

5. Take the necessary action.

There is another aspect you need to consider when putting a halt to your doubt. It is easy for the mind to continue to run in circles even after you've decided on your action plan. The only way to stop this circle of doubt is to be mindful of when you slip into this cycle. When you do, stop yourself immediately and reassure your mind that you have a plan in place that makes it no longer necessary to ponder the matter. Don't allow your mind to revert to replanning repeatedly; this can be a fruitless and highly draining cycle to be trapped in.

Affirmations

Regularly using positive affirmations is a wonderful way to increase your confidence and lower your anxiety levels. Use positive statements that are relevant to specific, current concerns. Phrase your affirmations clearly and directly, as this will make it easier to program your mind to not entertain worry and cause anxiety. You can opt to have a list of positive affirmations to help you better deal with stress and anxiety in your life.

Some examples of effective affirmations are

- I am feeling calm and relaxed.

- I am capable and confident.

- I am inhaling positivity and exhaling all my worries and concerns.

- I am good enough to achieve what I set out to do.

Using Diversions

Diversions can be an excellent way to direct your mind away from thoughts increasing your stress and anxiety. There are several ways to approach diversions, and I am sharing some example techniques. But first, I want us to explore precisely what diversion techniques entail.

Diversion Techniques Defined

Diversions serve as distractions to shift your focus away from the thoughts that keep your stress and anxiety levels elevated. It usually consists of a specific activity that will require you to break free from the downward spiral of your thoughts. This happens as you must think about something else while doing this activity. A popular diversion technique would be to have an elastic band around your wrist. Once you find yourself trapped in worrying, you would start snapping the band around your wrist. However, there are many other ways you would also be able to divert your thoughts.

The Five Best Diversion Techniques

These five techniques are, in my opinion, the most effective to divert your thoughts away from what causes your anxiety.

Find Something Entertaining to Do

You don't have to pick something that will keep you busy for long, as the purpose of a diversion technique is to distract you just long enough to calm yourself down. While a lot of the stress we are experiencing today is due to the fast-paced environment created by technology, our smart devices also offer a range of ways to distract our attention from our concerns. Some alternate activities are

- read a chapter or two
- watch some TV
- page through a magazine
- listen to music
- look at online video clips, listen to a podcast, or even a chapter in an audiobook
- play a game on your phone
- Remember that this shouldn't keep you gripped for long—the purpose is not to lower your productivity but to divert your attention to something else.

Showcase Your Creativity

Whether you are extremely creative or have only a few creative bones, immersing yourself in a creative task is an excellent distraction. Grab a pencil or a brush and create something beautiful. You can decide if you want to have a large creative project to work on whenever you feel stressed, or if you would only want to have a small project to keep you busy for a short while. Something as simple as having a book to doodle in can also be a helpful aid nearby.

Talk to Someone

A shared concern becomes half a concern. So, if something is troubling your mind, reach out to a trusted friend or family member and share your concerns. It will bring you great relief to get the matter off your mind, and the other person may even provide you with a fresh perspective.

Get Active

One of the best ways to get "good" hormones flowing and free your mind from anxiety, stress, and panic is to be active. Take a brisk walk around the block, or put on your shoes and go for a jog. As little as 20 minutes of exercise is enough to shift your state of mind from being anxious to feeling much calmer and more relaxed.

Pen Down Your Thoughts

When it comes to expressing our thoughts, there is nothing more patient than paper. By writing down all your concerns, you get them out of your system. You can free your mind and restore your calm state by expressing your negative thoughts. You can invest in a specific journal for this purpose or simply grab the closest piece of paper and start writing.

Takeaway

Experiencing high stress levels and anxiety can already be highly disruptive to your life. It only worsens the situation if you feel utterly helpless in your state. It is always good to have people to reach out to in your time of need. Yet, it is empowering to know that you have the necessary skills to overcome your challenges, even when they are at their worst. Every technique I've shared in this chapter holds the potential to grab you out of your anxious state. All you need to do is to repeat them often enough to master these skills. As you become more aware of how you can apply these coping mechanisms, you'll become more confident in what they can do for you. Eventually, they'll become part of your regular routines. This is when you'll employ them before your situation becomes so severe that it starts to feel like you've lost all control.

Leave a 1-Click Review

If you enjoyed this book, I would appreciate it if you could leave a brief review on Amazon, even if it is only a few sentences.

Reviews enable independent authors like me to reach the right audience and help more people like you.

Click here to Leave a Review

Outsmart Anxiety review page

Chapter Ten

Conclusion

The best way to overcome any obstacle is to familiarize ourselves with every aspect of the stumbling block ahead. This is where we had our entry point in this book. Before tackling our anxiety effectively, we must understand what it is and how it developed over time. Only once we have gained clarity on the causes of our anxiety and can identify the root of this concern can we eradicate it entirely from our lives.

The next stage is to explore the system within which the concern manifests. The human body is highly complex—the mind and body work closely together, impacting our overall state of being. While this interaction between mind and body can land us in a downward spiral, we can also utilize the connection to enjoy improvement and recovery. We've explored the mind–body connection and how something as physical as nutrition can benefit our mental state. Here, we delved deeper to determine what foods we should have more of and what we need to eliminate from our diets.

As humans, we are holistic beings; to address any specific concern, we would need a holistic approach. It is why we covered every possible treatment option we are able to follow. We explored medicine and how it can be beneficial, but also its limitations. I'll never deny that professional treatment is vital to the healing journey. Yet, while this will be highly beneficial to us, seeing a professional expert may not be enough.

Obviously, our support networks are also crucial to our recovery, but ultimately, how effective we'll be at claiming back our lives will depend on our own actions. Even if it doesn't feel this way, we remain in control. If we don't take up this power position, anxiety will. Therefore, I've shared many coping mechanisms which will all empower us to take control quickly once we feel our anxiety increase. It is how we can effectively restore our calm state of being. These techniques will also allow us to better manage our emotions.

Now, you are familiar with what is happening to you when it feels like your life is falling apart due to anxiety. Even better, though, is that you are equipped with all the necessary information and tools to ensure this doesn't happen. You have what it takes to reclaim your life. Use these tools and live your life to its full potential.

References

Images titled The Anxiety Habit Loop and The Impact of Diets on Gut Health provided by François J. Camus.

Aarons-Mele, M (Host). (2021, December 6). Anxiety is a habit (No. 10) [Audio Podcast Episode]. In The Anxious Achiever. Harvard Business Review. https://hbr.org/podcast/2021/12/anxiety-is-a-habit#:~:text=Just%20sitting%20there%20waiting%20for

Adam, B. (2021, June 18). How your lifestyle affects your mental health. Psychreg.

https://www.psychreg.org/lifestyle-affects-mental-health/

American Psychological Association. (n.d.). Anxiety. https://www.apa.org/topics/anxiety#:~:text=Anxiety%20is%20an%20emotion%20characterized

Anxiety & Depression Association of America. (n.d.-a). Anxiety disorders—Facts and statistics. https://adaa.org/understanding-anxiety/facts-statistics#:~:text=Facts%20and%20Statistics-

Anxiety & Depression Association of America. (n.d.-b). Exercise for stress and anxiety. https://adaa.org/living-with-anxiety/managing-anxiety/exercise-stress-and-anxiety

Azarian, B. (2019, March 26). How anxiety distorts your perception of the world. Psychology Today. https://www.psychologytoday.com/ca/blog/mind-in-the-machine/201903/how-anxiety-distorts-your-perception-the-world

Brewer, J. (2021). Unwinding anxiety: New science shows how to break the cycles of worry and fear to heal your mind. Avery.

Centers for Disease Control and Prevention. (n.d.). Anxiety and depression in children: Get the facts. U.S. Department of Health & Human Services. https://www.cdc.gov/childrensmentalhealth/features/anxiety-depression-children.html#:~:text=Anxiety%20and%20depression%20affect%20many

Center, K. (2021, March 18). Can watching the news cause depression? The Kimberly Center. https://kimberlycenter.com/mental-health/watching-the-news-and-mental-health/#:~:text=When%20you%20consume%20negative%20information

Clear, J. (2018). Atomic habits: An easy & proven way to build good habits & break bad ones. Avery.

Dattani, S., Ritchie, H., & Roser, M. (2021, August). Mental health. Our World in Data. https://ourworldindata.org/mental-health

Dutheil, S., Ota, K. T., Wohleb, E. S., Rasmussen, K., & Duman, R. S. (2015). High-fat diet induced anxiety and anhedonia: Impact on Brain homeostasis and inflammation. Neuropsychopharmacology, 41(7), 1874–1887. https://doi.org/10.1038/npp.2015.357

Fearless Motivation. (2015, September 7). The most amazing Dr. Wayne Dyer quotes & affirmations. https://www.fearlessmotivation.com/2015/09/07/the-most-amazing-dr-wayne-dyer-quotes-affirmations/

Frankl, V. E. (2006). Man's search for meaning. Beacon Press. (Original work published 1946)

Ghannoum, M. A., Ford, M., Bonomo, R. A., Gamal, A. & McCormick. T. S. (2021). A microbiome-driven approach to combating depression during the COVID-19 pandemic. Frontiers in Nutrition, 8, 672390, https://doi.org/10.3389/fnut.2021.672390

Hampton, D. (2016, March 20). Serotonin's role in depression and willpower (and how you can make more naturally). The Best Brain Possible. https://thebestbrainpossible.com/how-to-increase-serotonin/

Hanson, R., McKay, M., Davis, M., Eshlelman, E. R. (2020, September 25). One way to calm an anxious mind: Notice when you're doing OK. TED Conferences. https://ideas.ted.com/one-way-to-calm-an-anxious-mind-notice-when-youre-doing-ok/

Hargasova, L. (2020, February 26). Research paper: Neuroscience behind creating a habit—Simplified. International Coach Academy. https://coachcampus.com/coach-portfolios/research-papers/lucia-hargasova-neuroscience-behind-creating-a-habit-simplified/

Hart, P. (n.d.). What is the mind-body connection? University of Minnesota. https://www.takingcharge.csh.umn.edu/what-is-the-mind-body-connection

Harvard Health Publishing. (2021a, April 19). The gut-brain connection. https://www.health.harvard.edu/diseases-and-conditions/the-gut-brain-connection#:~:text=The%20gastrointestinal%20tract%20is%20sensitive

Harvard Health Publishing. (2021b, June 12). Yoga for better mental health. https://www.health.harvard.edu/staying-healthy/yoga-for-better-mental-health#:~:text=Improved%20mood&text=But%20yoga%20may%20have%20additional

Hill, D. (n.d.). Knowing others is intelligence, knowing yourself is true wisdom. Lifehack.

https://www.lifehack.org/535789/knowing-others-intelligence-knowing-yourself-true-wisdom

Holder, M. K., Peters, N. V., Whylings, J., Fields, C. T., Gewirtz, A. T., Chassaing, B., & de Vries, G. J. (2019). Dietary emulsifiers consumption alters anxiety-like and social-related behaviors in mice in a sex-dependent manner. Scientific Reports, 9(1). https://doi.org/10.1038/s41598-018-36890-3

Holland, M. (2022, June 22). 6 options for anxiety therapy. Choosing Therapy. https://www.choosingtherapy.com/anxiety-therapy/

Jagoo, K. (2021, August 25). Even with exercise, sedentary lifestyle has consequences for mental health. Verywell Mind. https://www.verywellmind.com/study-suggests-sitting-has-negative-impact-on-mental-health-5195714

Jeffrey, S. (2018, December 2). A complete guide to changing your fixed mindset into a growth mindset. Scott Jeffrey. https://scottjeffrey.com/change-your-fixed-mindset/

Khurana, R. (n.d.). A psychiatrist explains anxiety medications. Seattle Anxiety Specialists, PLLC: Psychiatry & Psychotherapy. https://seattleanxiety.com/blog/2019/6/27/a-psychiatrist-explains-anxiety-medications

Lillard, A. S., & Erisir, A. (2011). Old dogs learning new tricks: Neuroplasticity beyond the juvenile period. Developmental Review, 31(4), 207–239. https://doi.org/10.1016/j.dr.2011.07.008

Lin, K., Li, Y., Toit, E. D., Wendt, L., & Sun, J. (2021). Effects of polyphenol supplementations on improving depression, anxiety, and quality of life in patients with depression. Frontiers in Psychiatry, 12. https://doi.org/10.3389/fpsyt.2021.765485

Marks, J. (2021, October 8). Grounding exercises: Using your 5 senses for anxiety relief. Psych Central. https://psychcentral.com/anxiety/using-the-five-senses-for-anxiety-relief

Mayer, E. A. (2018). The mind-gut connection: How the hidden conversation within our bodies impacts our mood, our choices, and our overall health. Harper Wave.

Mcleod, S. (2021). Pavlov's dogs study and Pavlovian conditioning explained. Simply Psychology. https://www.simplypsychology.org/pavlov.html#:~:text=Pavlov%20showed%20that%20dogs%20could

Meg. (2022, March 21). Protein & anxiety: What to know & what sources to include? Meg de Jong Nutrition. https://megdejongnutrition.com/protein-anxiety-what-to-know-what-sources-to-include/

Micronutrients as a treatment for anxiety & depression. (2018, October 15). Hardy Nutritionals. https://www.hardynutritionals.com/blog/2018/10/micronutrients-for-anxiety-and-depression

Morales-Brown, L. (2021, January 19). What does it mean to be "touch starved"? Medical News Today. https://www.medicalnewstoday.com/articles/touch-starved

Nabil, S. (2017, July 27). Why medication alone isn't enough to treat your anxiety. GoodTherapy. https://www.goodtherapy.org/blog/why-medication-alone-isnt-enough-to-treat-your-anxiety-0727175

Nall, R. (2019, April 1). What are the benefits of sunlight? Healthline. https://www.healthline.com/health/depression/benefits-sunlight

National Alliance on Mental Illness. (2017, December). Anxiety disorders. https://www.nami.org/About-Mental-Illness/Mental-Health-Conditions/Anxiety-Disorders#:~:text=Over%2040%20million%20adults%20in

National Human Genome Research Institute. (2022, October 20). Microbiome. U.S. Department of Health & Human Services, National Institutes of Health. https://www.genome.gov/genetics-glossary/Microbiome

National Institute of Mental Health. (n.d.). Any anxiety disorder. U.S. Department of Health & Human Services, National Institutes of Health. https://www.nimh.nih.gov/health/statistics/any-anxiety-disorder

Orloff, J. (2011, April 11). Are you addicted to anxiety? Learn how not to be. Psychology Today. https://www.psychologytoday.com/ca/blog/emotional-freedom/201104/are-you-addicted-anxiety-learn-how-not-be#:~:text=To%20quiet%20anxiety%20and%20turn

Plano, C. (n.d.). You are the average of the five people you spend time with. Ellevate. https://www.ellevatenetwork.com/articles/9895-you-are-the-average-of-the-five-people-you-spend-time-with

A quote by Isabel Allende. (n.d.). Goodreads. https://www.goodreads.com/quotes/79570-we-only-have-what-we-give

A quote from Max Planck. (n.d.). Goodreads. https://www.goodreads.com/quotes/379714-science-cannot-solve-the-ultimate-mystery-of-nature-and-that

A quote by Śāntideva. (n.d.). Goodreads. https://www.goodreads.com/quotes/234528-if-the-problem-can-be-solved-why-worry-if-the

A quote by Sherry A. Rogers. (n.d.). Goodreads. https://www.goodreads.com/quotes/517950-the-road-to-health-is-paved-with-good-intestines

A quote by Will Durant. (n.d.). BrainyQuote. https://www.brainyquote.com/quotes/will_durant_145967

A quote by Will Hurd. (n.d.). BrainyQuote. https://www.brainyquote.com/quotes/will_hurd_1034725

Ratey, J. J. (2019, October 24). Can exercise help treat anxiety? Harvard Health Publishing. https://www.health.harvard.edu/blog/can-exercise-help-treat-anxiety-2019102418096

Remes, O. (2017). How to cope with anxiety [Video]. TED Conferences. https://www.ted.com/talks/olivia_remes_how_to_cope_with_anxiety?language=en

Rinninella, E., Cintoni, M., Raoul, P., Lopetuso, L. R., Scaldaferri, F., Pulcini, G., Miggiano, G. A. D., Gasbarrini, A., & Mele, M. C. (2019). Food components and dietary habits: Keys for a healthy gut microbiota composition. Nutrients, 11(10), 2393. https://doi.org/10.3390/nu11102393

Roberts, N. F. (2019, December 4). Psychological research explains why TV viewing is higher than ever. Forbes. https://www.forbes.com/sites/nicolefisher/2019/12/04/psychological-research-explains-why-tv-viewing-is-higher-than-ever/?sh=774d2b813b0b

Robertson, R. (2020, August 20). The gut-brain connection: How it works and the role of nutrition. Healthline. https://www.healthline.com/nutrition/gut-brain-connection

Scott, E. (2022, May 11). What is eustress? Verywell Mind. https://www.verywellmind.com/what-you-need-to-know-about-eustress-3145109

Star, K. (2020, September 17). The benefits of anxiety and nervousness. Verywell Mind. https://www.verywellmind.com/benefits-of-anxiety-2584134

Surprising facts about phobias. (n.d.). Aruma. https://www.aruma.com.au/about-us/blog/surprising-facts-about-phobias/#:~:text=There%20are%20more%20than%20400

Walton, A. G. (2015, February 9). 7 ways meditation can actually change the brain. Forbes. https://www.forbes.com/sites/alicegwalton/2015/02/09/7-ways-meditation-can-actually-change-the-brain/?sh=1ff708561465

Wellness, B. (2019, August 15). Five ways to influence your subconscious mind & transform your life. Bhakti Wellness Center. https://bhakticlinic.com/subconscious-mind-transform-life/

Leave a 1-Click Review

If you liked this book, I would be incredibly thankful if you could take a minute to leave a brief review on Amazon, even just a few sentences.

Reviews help independent authors like myself get in front of the right audience and help more people like you.

Click here to Leave a Review

Made in United States
Troutdale, OR
02/15/2025

28990575R00097